# MIND YOUR ENGLISH

## SERIES 1

## Improve on Your English Sentences

MAGNUS OKU

ISBN: 9789785559606

# TABLE OF CONTENTS

# INTRODUCTION

Language serves as a powerful tool of expression, encompassing both verbal and written communication. The English language, rich in morphological, syntactic, phonological, and semantic nuances, relies on a structured grammar to convey meaning effectively. This grammar extends to the arrangement of words, phrases, clauses, and sentences, governed by rules that facilitate the creation of coherent and meaningful expressions.

According to Fromkin and Rodman (1983: 110), individuals proficient in a language possess a vast repository of words, with sounds and meanings ingrained through practical usage. While there exist historical, social, cultural, and regional variations in English, this book elucidates a generalized form of present-day Standard English. This standardized variant finds application in public discourse, spanning areas such as broadcasting, education, entertainment, and government, encompassing both formal and informal speech – emphasizing correct usage.

Every word in a language assumes the form of either a free morphological entity or a product resulting from the combination of various components. The assignment of functions to these words by language speakers forms the basis of word classes or parts of speech, including nouns, verbs, adjectives, adverbs, pronouns, prepositions, conjunctions, and interjections.

While variations in grammar exist between the standard forms of British English, American English, and Australian English, these discrepancies are subtle when compared to lexical and pronunciation differences.

Recognizing dictionaries as repositories of words at a specific time, it's essential to acknowledge their limitations in encapsulating the entirety of a language's vocabulary. New words continually integrate into a language through inventions, discoveries, neologisms, private poetic creations, and morphological processes like affixation and compounding. Consequently, dictionaries undergo regular revisions to remain current, urging users to consult updated versions for optimal relevance.

The intricate network of words reveals their existence within sets known as synonyms, sharing core meanings while varying based on general/specific meaning, syntactic category, association, semantic fields, tenor, and mode. When confronted with the challenge of choosing from this array of words, the concept of 'diction' emerges. Users choose their words based on different things like purpose, context, and what fits the situation, showing how language works in many ways in human expression.

# FOREWORD

In the vast landscape of English language education, where countless textbooks vie for attention, Magnus Oku presents a refreshing and accessible approach in Mind Your English Series I. In a world where proficiency in English is not just a skill but a necessity, this series stands out, offering students a clear and comprehensible guide to discerning correctness from error.

As you delve into the pages of this unique publication, it becomes evident that it is unlike traditional textbooks. It resembles a blend of a dictionary and a telephone directory, reminiscent of the trusted Students Companion from bygone days. This nostalgic nod echoes the pedagogical methods of the 1960s, drawing parallels to the teachings of luminaries like Mrs. Reeds at Igbaja Teachers Training College in Kwara State, who instilled in her students a mastery of common errors, controlled composition, and phonetics.

Mind Your English Series I serves a dual purpose – it can be an independent reference guide or seamlessly integrated into coursework, seminars, or workshops to complement other English language teaching materials. Magnus Oku's approach, steeped in simplicity and effectiveness, promises to demystify the intricacies of English, empowering learners to navigate the language with confidence.

**Prof. Jonathan Aremu FMR**
**Vice Chancellor, Covenant University**
**Regional Expert ECOWAS Commission, Abuja**

# SEGMENT 1

## ENGLISH SENTENCES

Knowing how to speak and write English correctly opens many opportunities even for jobs and improves social status. This book provides an overview of common English sentence structures. The book differs from traditional books on English grammar by providing formal descriptions that will enable a student of English to generate correctly formed sentences easily. Persons studying English as a second language (ESL) or those who would like to use English language interfaces in computer-based applications will find this approach particularly useful because it avoids the ambiguities encountered in traditional English grammars. The description uses the notation below.

### Sentence Types

English has four main sentence types by function:

**Declarative Sentences:** used to form statements. Examples: "Mary is here.", "My name is Mary."

**Interrogative Sentences:** used to ask questions. Examples: "Where is Mary?", "What is your name?"

**Imperative Sentences**: used to give commands. Examples: "Come here." "Tell me your name."

**Exclamatory Sentences:** used to express strong emotions. Examples: "What a wonderful feeling that was!", "How on Earth did I read that!"

## Basic English Sentence Structures: Parts of speech

Sentences are made up of words that belong to different groups based on their function. The word "fire," for example, can be a noun or a verb depending on how it is used.

**Noun**: "The fire burned the building."

**Verb:** "Fire the gun. "On Writing Complete, Grammatically Correct Sentences

- Sentence Fragments
- Run-on Sentences
- Subject-Verb Agreement
- Parallel Structure

There are four main problems that prevent people from writing complete, grammatically correct sentences. These problems include:

**(a)** The Sentence Fragment; **(b)** The Run-On Sentence; **(c)** Lack Of Subject- Verb And Pronoun-Reference Agreement; and **(d)** Lack Of Parallel Structure.

## Sentence Fragments

A fragment is a sentence which is not complete, and therefore not grammatically correct. Sentence fragments are problematic because they are disjointed and confusing to the reader. There are three main causes of fragments: (a) a missing subject; (b) a missing verb; (c) "danger" words which are not finished.

There are three ways to check for sentence completeness:

**1. Find the subject.** A subject is the noun or pronoun about which something is written. To find the subject of a sentence, identify who or what is doing the action. If there is no subject, the sentence is a fragment. Consider the two examples below.

"The student felt nervous before the speech."

"Thought about leaving the room."

The first sentence above is complete, because it contains both a subject and a verb. The subject of this sentence is the student. The sentence contains a subject which answers the question, "who or what felt nervous?"

The second sentence is a fragment, because there is no identifiable subject. The sentence does not contain a subject which answers the question, "who or what thought about leaving?" To correct the second sentence, one could write: "He thought about leaving the room." Alternatively, one could combine the two sentences to form one complete sentence: "

The student felt nervous before the speech and thought about leaving the room."

**2. Find the verb**. A verb is the action word in a sentence. Verbs express action, existence or occurrence. To find the verb in a sentence, identify what happened. If there is no identifiable action, the sentence is a fragment. Consider the two examples below:

"Many scientists think in strange ways. Einstein, for example."
"Many scientists, such as Einstein, think in strange ways."

The first example above has one complete sentence followed by a fragment. "Einstein, for example" is a fragment because there is no verb. "Einstein" serves as the subject (he is the one doing something), but the rest of the sentence does not express what action he is taking.

The second example is a complete sentence. In this case, the sentence contains both a subject (scientists) and a verb (think). Alternatively, one could write the following: "Many scientists think in strange ways. Einstein, for example, could not tolerate more than one bar of soap in his home." In this case, there are two complete sentences. In the second sentence, the subject is Einstein, and the verb is "could not tolerate."

**3. Check for "danger" words**. A danger word is one that starts a thought but needs a follow-up phrase to complete it. These words are sometimes called "cliffhangers" because they begin a statement but leave it unfinished. Here are some examples:

"If you come home..."

"When the rain falls..."

"Because he is mean..."

In these sentences, the danger words are "if," "when," and "because." When these words are used at the beginning of a phrase, they need a follow-up to complete the idea.

**Example:**

**Incorrect:** *If you come home on time... then what?*

**Correct:** *If you come home on time, I will buy you a present.*

**Incorrect:** *When it rains... what happens?*

**Correct:** *When it rains, the gutters become clogged.*

**Incorrect:** *Because he is mean... what is the result?*

**Correct:** *Because he is mean, I will not take a class from him.*

Danger words can be useful in writing, but it's important to make sure the sentence has a clear ending. Some common danger words include after, unless, although, how, as if, when, because, where, before, while, if, until, once, so that, since, whether. Always ensure these sentences are complete by adding a concluding phrase.

## Run-on Sentences

A run-on sentence is one which contains two (or more) complete sentences without the proper punctuation to create separate sentences. There are two common forms of the run-on: (1) the "comma splice" in which a comma is inserted between two complete sentences where a period should be used; (2) a lack of punctuation where a semi-colon or period is needed.

**Incorrect Examples - The Comma Splice**

John is a musician; he plays the guitar for a living. The girl walked home; she decided not to ride the bus. He could only guess at the number of guests who attended the party, the entire yard was filled with people.

In the examples above, the sentences are incorrectly joined by a comma, thus "splicing" two complete sentences together into one run-on sentence. To correct these run-on's, the comma should be replaced by a period, thus creating two separate sentences, as shown below.

**Correct Examples**

John is a musician. He plays the guitar for a living. The girl walked home. She decided not to ride the bus. He could only guess at the number of guests who attended the party. The entire yard was filled with people.

**Incorrect Examples - Lack of Punctuation**

There is a problem with the television; however, no one is available to fix it.

Nobody knows what really happened. The policeman said there was a fight.

That is the problem; when people have conflict, they attack each other personally.

In each of the examples above, punctuation is needed to separate the two parts of the sentence, such as a semi-colon or a period.

**Correct Examples**

There is a problem with the television; however, no one is available to fix it.

There is a problem with the television. However, no one is available to fix it.

Nobody knows what really happened; the policeman said there was a fight.

Nobody knows what really happened. The policeman said there was a fight.

That is the problem when people have conflict; they attack each other personally.

That is the problem when people have conflict. They attack each other personally.

## Subject-Verb Agreement

For a sentence to be grammatically correct, the subject and verb must both be singular or plural.

In other words, the subject and verb must agree with one another in their tense. If the subject is in plural form, the verb should also be in plural form (and vice versa). To ensure subject-verb agreement, identify the main subject and verb in the sentence, then check to see if they are both singular or plural. Consider the examples below.

**Incorrect examples - Subject-Verb Agreement**

- "A recipe with more than six ingredients are too complicated."

  The main subject in this sentence is "recipe," which is singular. The main verb is "are," which is plural.

- "The facts in that complex case is questionable."

  The main subject in this sentence is "facts," which is plural. The main verb, "is," is singular.

- "The people is wearing formal attires."

The main subject in this sentence is "people," which is plural. The main verb is "is wearing," which is singular.

**Correct examples**

- "A recipe with more than six ingredients is too complicated."
- "The facts in that complex case are questionable."
- "The people are wearing formal attires."

A variation of the subject-verb agreement is **pronoun-reference agreement**. In the case of pronoun-reference agreement, the pronoun and its antecedent should agree with one another in singular or plural form. Consider the examples below.

**Incorrect examples - Pronoun-Reference Agreement**

- "A manager should always be honest with their employees."

  The subject in this sentence, "manager," is singular. The corresponding pronoun, "their," is plural.

- "Organizations must be careful about discriminating against its employees."

  The subject in this sentence is "organizations," which is plural. The corresponding pronoun, "its," is singular.

- "If you really care about somebody, let them make their own choices."

In this sentence, the pronoun "somebody" is singular, but the corresponding pronouns, "them" and "their," are plural.

**Correct examples**

- "A manager should always be honest with his (or her) employees."
- "Organizations must be careful about discriminating against their employees."
- "If you really care about somebody, let him (or her) make his (or her) own choices."

## Parallel Structure

Parallel structure in a sentence refers to the extent to which different parts of the sentence match each other in form. When more than one phrase or description is used in a sentence, those phrases or descriptions should be consistent in form and wording. Parallel structure is important because it enhances the ease with which the reader can follow the writer's idea. Consider the following examples.

**Incorrect examples - Parallel Structure**

- **Example One:** "He is strong and a tough competitor."

  Notice that "strong" and "a tough competitor" are not in the same form.

- **Example Two:** "The new coach is a smart strategist, an effective manager, and works hard."

  Notice that "a smart strategist" and "an effective manager" are consistent with one another, but not consistent with "works hard."

- **Example Three:** "In the last minute of the game, John intercepted the football, evaded the tacklers, and a touchdown was scored."

  Notice that the first two phrases in this sentence are consistent with one another: "intercepted the football" and "evaded the tacklers." However, the final phrase, "and a touchdown was scored," is not consistent with the first two phrases.

**Correct examples**

- **Example One:** "He is strong and competitive."
- **Example Two:** "The new coach is a smart strategist, an effective manager, and a hard worker."
- **Example Three:** "In the last minute of the game, John intercepted the football, evaded the tacklers, and scored a touchdown."

# SEGMENT 2

## Common Mistakes (Checklist 1)

Below is a list of the most common English language mistakes occurring in student papers. These expressions constitute misapplied notions and must be avoided in the use of English.

| S/N | Incorrect | Correct |
|---|---|---|
| 1 | I cracked my brain to solve the mathematical problem.<br>***Cracked means broken.** | I racked my brains to solve the mathematical problem.<br>***She racked her brains trying to remember exactly what she ate.**<br>***Rack means to think very hard or for a long time about something.** |
| 2 | I was lying in the bed when he came in. | I was lying in bed when he came in. |
| 3 | Please off-load the goods. | Please unload the vehicle. |
| 4 | The teacher asked me what my names were. | The teacher asked me what my name was. |
| 5 | Enough is enough. | It is enough. |
| 6 | The scissors is on the table. | The scissors are on the table.<br>***A pair of scissors is on the table.** |
| 7 | I came with my car. | I came in my car.<br>I came on my bicycle.<br>I am on business. |
| 8 | I am in business. | I am on business. |
| 9 | This is Charles' car.<br>This is Charles car. | This is Charles's car. |
| 10 | Give me this book for goodness' sake. | Give me this book for goodness' sake.<br>Give me this book for heaven's sake. |
| 11 | I came by 10:00am in the morning. | I came at 10:00am. |
| 12 | Please return back the book. | Please return the book. |
| 13 | Drop me a note by today. | Please drop by to see me today.<br>Drop in (do) to see me. |
| 14 | How many years did I carry and study law?<br>I will offload the junction. | How old are you in law?<br>I will alight at the junction. |
| 15 | Drive over your car for me to pass. | Please pull over your car.<br>Please drive off to the side. |
| 16 | James is an expert in driving. | James is an expert at driving.<br>He is more expert at flying. |

| | | |
|---|---|---|
| 17 | Sit more nearer to your elbow. | Sit nearer to your elbow. |
| 18 | Each and everyone should come. | Everyone should come.<br>Each person should come. |
| 19 | NEPA has done the fault. | There was a power outage/failure. |
| 20 | All of us up and down. | All of us rose up. |
| 21 | Call off something. | Call it off. |
| 22 | Do not put your mouth in this matter. | Keep silent.<br>Do not interfere in this matter. |
| 23 | I am feeling cold. | I feel cold. |
| 24 | He did not give me an up-to-date information. | He did not give me up-to-date information. |
| 25 | As I said earlier on.... | As I said earlier.... |
| 26 | Practicalize what you have learnt. | Put what you have learnt into practice |
| 27 | I don't know offhead how more I made last week. | I don't know offhand how more I made last week.<br>I know your phone number by heart. |
| 28 | He is walking under the sun/rain.<br>**Note**: According to the Oxford Dictionary of Current English, "under the sun" is an idiomatic expression used to emphasize that you are talking about a very large number of things. E.g. we talked about everything under the sun. | He is walking in the sun/rain. |
| 29 | He scaled through the exams. | He sailed through the exam. |
| 30 | Less the noise. | Don't make so much noise. |
| 31 | A beggar has no choice. | Beggars cannot be choosers. |
| 32 | I will pay you a visit next tomorrow. | I will pay you a visit the day after tomorrow. |
| 33 | You forgot your phone | You left your phone. |
| 34 | Presently, he is the chairman of the board. | At present, he is the chairman of the board.<br>I will be with you presently. |
| 35 | Your work is more perfect than mine. | Your work is perfect. |
| 36 | Obi said bye-bye to his elder sister. | Obi said good-bye to his elder sister. |
| 37 | Queen is more taller than Linda. | Queen is taller than Linda. |
| 38 | I prefer rice than beans. | I prefer rice to beans. |
| 39 | I have been here since two weeks.<br>**Note**: since is used when definite reference is implied while for is used when | I have been here for two weeks.<br>I have been teaching English since 1980. |

| | | |
|---|---|---|
| | duration is implied. | |
| 40 | They elected him as the chairman. | They elected him chairman. |
| 41 | Members treat one another like brothers and are bounded by oath. | Members treat one another like brothers and are bound by Oath. |
| 42 | This door is out of bound. | This door is out of bounds. |
| 43 | The money was divided between the five sons. | The money was divided among the five sons. |
| 44 | Borrow me your book, please. | Lend me your book. |
| 45 | I agree with your plan for saving money. | I agree to your plan for saving money.<br>The members agree with the president. |
| 46 | I came with my pen/bag. | I brought my pen/bag.<br>I came with John. |
| 47 | Efe sat besides her father. | Efe sat beside her father.<br>There were four persons besides Queen in the boat. |
| 48 | They discussed about the plan.<br>**Note**: Discuss means to exchange ideas about something. | They discussed the plan. |
| 49 | He waved me. | He waved at me. |
| 50 | Kelechi has an edge over others. | Kelechi has an edge on others. |
| 51 | The fish weighed around five kilograms. | The fish weighed about five kilograms. |
| 52 | John disvirgined Judith yesterday. | John deflowered Judith yesterday. |
| 53 | This is raining season. | This is rainy season. |
| 54 | The expiring data of the drug is written. | The expiry data of the drug is written. |
| 55 | I am not understanding you. | I cannot understand you. |
| 56 | Please shake me. | Please shake my hands<br>Shake hands with me. |
| 57 | Please sign your signature here. | Please sign your name here.<br>Please put your signature here.<br>Please append your signature here. |
| 58 | John has disposed the goods. | John has disposed of the goods. |
| 59 | Please clean the board. | Please wipe off the chalkboard. |
| 60 | I have told you time without number to leave me alone. | I have told you times without number to leave me alone. |
| 61 | Presently, he lives at Lagos. | At present, he lives in Lagos. |
| 62 | You did not approve my leaving school this year. | You did not approve of my leaving school this year. |
| 63 | I am doing this because of you | I am doing this in your interest |

| | | |
|---|---|---|
| 64 | I will pay you a visit next tomorrow. | I will pay you a visit the day after tomorrow. |
| 65 | I shall see you by sunrise. | I shall see you at sunrise. |
| 66 | Mr. John became the principal of the college in 1928. | Mr. John became principal of the college in 1928. |
| 67 | I was there on 3:00pm. | I was there at 3:00. |
| 68 | I am looking forward to hear from you. | I am looking forward to hearing from you. |
| 69 | I came with a view of seeing you. | I came with a view to seeing you. |
| 70 | The question reoccurred throughout the book. | The question recurred throughout the book. |
| 71 | My wife has delivered a baby. | My wife was delivered of a baby. |
| 72 | This is a day and half job. | This is day and half's job. |
| 73 | I deal on electronics. | I deal in electronics. |
| 74 | The boy is putting on trousers. | The boy is putting on a pair of trousers. |
| 75 | I want to check my mails. | I want to check my mail. |
| 76 | He used my towel to clean his body after having his bath. | He used my towel to rub his body after having his bath. |
| 77 | If rain should fall, I would not come. | If it should rain, I would not come. |
| 78 | Celestine is my junior brother. | Celestine is my younger brother. Celestine is a junior officer. |
| 79 | Let me give you an advice. | Let me give you a piece of advice.<br>I strongly advise against going out on your own. |
| 80 | I am in a haste. | I am in haste.<br>I am in a hurry. |
| 81 | I am coming (while you are leaving for somewhere). | I will be back (while you are leaving for somewhere). |
| 82 | I came with leg. | I came on foot. |
| 83 | You have longer throat. | You have a voracious appetite. |
| 84 | She lives in the campus.<br>She lives inside the campus. | She lives on campus. |
| 85 | Off/on the television set/tap. | Turn off/on the television set. |
| 86 | Is John in the office? I think. | Is John in the Office? I think so. |
| 87 | Julius has been pursuing Princess for months. | Julius has been chasing after Princess for months. |
| 88 | I must have to go to school. | I must go to school.<br>I have to go to school. |
| 89 | Any question?<br>Any problem? | Is there any question?<br>Do you have any problem? |
| 90 | I watched the programme in the television. | I watched the programme on the television. |
| 91 | John is insultive.<br>She was really insultive to me. | John is insulting.<br>She was really insulting to me. |

| | | |
|---|---|---|
| 92 | I will see you in a twinkle of an eye. | I will see you in the twinkle of an eye. |
| 93 | I congratulate you for your success. | I congratulate you on your success. |
| 94 | Rice and stew are ready. | Rice and stew is ready. |
| 95 | One should be careful with himself. | One should be careful with oneself. You should be careful with yourself. |
| 96 | Delivery is without charge. | Delivery is free of charge. |
| 97 | They should mind theirselves. | They should mind themselves. |
| 98 | Do not shout on me. | Do not shout at me. |
| 99 | Stella is calling you (when Stella want to see the person). | Stella wants to see you. |
| 100 | She is a talkative. | She is a talker.<br>She is in a talkative mood. |
| 101 | I am disappointed at you. | I am disappointed in you.<br>I am disappointed at the result of the game. |
| 102 | It has tayed since day break. | It has been long since the break of the dawn |
| 103 | This is my first time of coming here. | I have been here for the first time. |
| 104 | Who is with my ruler. | Who has my ruler. |
| 105 | Where are you since. | Where have you been. |
| 106 | He is lacking blood. | He is short of blood. |
| 107 | Wait for. | Wait for me. |
| 108 | You are lacking behind. | You are lagging behind. |
| 109 | He is learning driving. | He is learning how to drive. |
| 110 | This is half current. | There is low voltage. |
| 111 | | |
| 112 | The food is very good.<br>He is a very good player . | The food is delicious.<br>He is a talented player. |
| 113 | Come rainfall or sunshine, I will jog. | Come rain or shine, I will jog. |
| 114 | He jumped out from the window. | He jumped out of the window. |
| 115 | We want the players to have the best education.<br>I will do my best to help you. | We want the players to have the best possible education.<br>I will do my best possible to help you. |
| 116 | He and me are friends. | He and I are friends. |
| 117 | The five boys liked each other. | The five boys liked one other.<br>The two boys liked each other. |

| | | |
|---|---|---|
| 118 | I don't hear Igbo. | I don't understand Igbo. |
| 119 | There are gallops in the road. | There are potholes in the road. |
| 120 | I went for the wake keeping. | I went for the burial wake. |
| 121 | My leg is scratching me. | My leg is itching me. |
| 122 | The corpers are here. | The corps members are here. |
| 123 | We received a letter from him of recent. | We received a letter from him recently. |
| 124 | He was arrested for bridge of contract. | He was arrested for breach of contract. |
| 125 | He contacted a disease. | He contracted a disease. |
| 126 | It rained continually for three hours (when there was no stop of the down pour). | It rained continuously for three hours (without stop or break). |
| 127 | Celestine's mother is a black while his father is a white. | Celestine is a mulatto. |
| 128 | He has his masters in education. | He has his master's in education. |
| 129 | He was out when I checked him. | He was out when I called to see him. |
| 130 | She has a bad colour. | She has a bad complexion. |
| 131 | I saw him at the bend corner of my street. | I saw him at the corner of my street. |
| 132 | Please dress let me sit down.<br>May I sit down here? | Please shit for me to sit.<br>May I sit here? |
| 133 | They have reached the linta level of the house. | They have reached the lintel level of the house. |
| 134 | He has open teeth. | He has diastema. |
| 135 | He should expantiate on what he said. | He should expatiate on what he said. |
| 136 | John did not compasate me. | John did not compensate me. |
| 137 | I had a big wound in the accident. | I sustained a serious injury in the accident.<br>I had a wound as a result of scratching the insect bite on my arms. |

# SEGMENT 3

## Common Mistakes (Checklist 2)

The errors are arranged into grammatical categories. Study the list and avoid making the same mistakes yourselves.

Misuse of the definite article "the": Abstract nouns do not normally take the definite article when used in general.

| Correct | Incorrect |
|---|---|
| 'The gang cannot distinguish Good from Evil' | 'The gang cannot distinguish **the** Good from **the** Evil' |
| 'She is afraid to enter/of entering the house to face reality' | 'She is afraid to enter the house, to face **the** reality' |
| 'He prefers to live close to nature because he is afraid of death' | 'He prefers to live close to **the** nature because he is afraid of **the** death' |

**Note:** Throughout this section, the correct expressions/usages are in the columns aligned to the left while the incorrect expressions/usages are alligned to the right.

## Prepositions:

**'At' after 'come':**

| Incorrect | Correct |
|---|---|
| They come home | They come at home |

**'With' instead of 'to':**

| Incorrect | Correct |
|---|---|
| Daisy is married to Tom | Daisy is married with Tom |

**'To' instead of 'with':**

| Incorrect | Correct |
|---|---|
| The problem I am confronted with... | The problem I am confronted to... |

**'During' instead of 'for':**

| Incorrect | Correct |
|---|---|
| She has not seen her son for eight years | She has not seen her son during eight years |

**'Since' instead of 'for':**

| Incorrect | Correct |
|---|---|
| They have known each other for eight years | They have known each other since eight years |

**'In the whole of' instead of 'throughout':**

| Incorrect | Correct |
|---|---|
| Throughout the story… | In the whole story… |

**'In' instead of 'inside':**

| Incorrect | Correct |
|---|---|

| | |
|---|---|
| She is unaware of the conflict happening inside her | She is unaware of the conflict happening in her |

**'In' instead of 'into':**

| Incorrect | Correct |
|---|---|
| She only wants to get into her son's room | She only wants to get in her son's room |

**'As' instead of 'like':**

| Incorrect | Correct |
|---|---|
| She felt like a stranger | She felt as a stranger |

**'Of' instead of 'with':**

| Incorrect | Correct |
|---|---|
| They cause Mrs. Carvacco to be disgusted with herself | They cause Mrs. Carvacco to be disgusted of herself |

**'Of' instead of 'by':**

| Incorrect | Correct |
|---|---|
| In this story by Doris Lessing… | In this story of Doris Lessing… |

**'OF' instead of 'for':**

| Incorrect | Correct |
|---|---|
| "I think there are two reasons for the fact that she decides to clear the room" | "I think there are two reasons of the fact that she decides to clear the room" |
| "She feels confused, and the reason for this is to be found in…" | "She feels confused, and the reason of this is to be found in…" |

**'That' instead of 'as':**

| Incorrect | Correct |
|---|---|
| "The second waiter feels the same as the old man" | "The second waiter feels the same that the old man" |

**'To' instead of 'with' after 'confront':**

| Incorrect | Correct |
|---|---|
| "They are confronted with an inextricable situation" | "They are confronted to an inextricable situation" |

**'To' instead of 'at' after 'arrive':**

| Incorrect | Correct |
|---|---|
| "She must arrive at a decision" | "She must arrive to a decision" |

**'Explain' without 'to':**

| Incorrect | Correct |
|---|---|
| "This story explains to us how we must look beyond the appearance of things" | "This story explains us how we must look beyond the appearance of things" |

**'Said' without 'to':**

| Incorrect | Correct |
| --- | --- |
| "He said to him/told him that he liked the house" | "He said him that he liked the house" |

**'Present' without 'with':**

| Incorrect | Correct |
| --- | --- |
| "John O'Hara presents us with the evolution of a mother's state of mind" | "John O'Hara presents us the evolution of a mother's state of mind" |

## Pronouns:

**'Him/her' instead of 'himself/herself' (when the object and the subject are the same person):**

| Incorrect | Correct |
| --- | --- |
| "She sees herself from a certain distance" | "She sees her from a certain distance" |

**'Who' (personal pronoun) instead of 'which' (impersonal pronoun):**

| Incorrect | Correct |
| --- | --- |
| "The wolf, which is a wild animal…" | "The wolf, who is a wild animal…" |

**'The one of' instead of 'that of':**

| Incorrect | Correct |
|---|---|
| "Mrs. Okoro's behaviour is that of a depressed person" | "Mr. Okoro's behaviour is the one of a depressed person" |
| "The third image is that of the magazine" | "The third image is the one of the magazine" |

## Negation:

**'Also not' instead of 'nor':**

| Incorrect | Correct |
|---|---|
| "He felt no qualm of conscience, nor any regret" | "He felt no qualm of conscience, and also not any regret" |

**Not anymore' instead of 'no longer':**

| Incorrect | Correct |
|---|---|
| "She must go back home because it is no longer possible to stay in France" | "She must go back home because it is not possible anymore to stay in France" |

## Verb forms:

**Inconsistent tenses:**

| Incorrect | Correct |
|---|---|
| "Her stepfather often comes to see her. One day he asks her…" | "Her stepfather often comes to see her. One day he asked her…" |

---

**Use of the present continuous instead of the present simple:**

| Incorrect | Correct |
|---|---|
| "The atmosphere is tense and the author intensifies it further with words like…" | "The atmosphere is tense and the author is still intensifying it with words like…" |

**Use of the infinitive instead of the present participle:**

| Incorrect | Correct |
|---|---|
| "This is a way to protect herself and to avoid showing what she really feels" | "This is a way to protect herself and to avoid to show what she really feels" |
| "This shows that she is not used to going into her son's room" | "This shows that she is not used to go into her son's room" |

**Use of the present participle instead of the infinitive:**

| Incorrect | Correct |
|---|---|
| "This scene explains her decision to get rid of Harry's belongings" | "This scene explains her decision of getting rid of Harry's belongings" |

**Use of a 'that' sub clause instead of the infinitive:**

| Incorrect | Correct |
|---|---|
| He would like the old man to leave | He would like **that** the old man leaves |
| She wants them to know | She wants **that** they know |

**'Can' instead of 'may'?**

| Incorrect | Correct |
|---|---|
| When we watch movies, we may or may not identify with the characters | When we watch movies, we can or cannot identify with the characters |

**Use of the present tense instead of the present perfect:**

| Incorrect | Correct |
|---|---|

| | |
|---|---|
| Jim and Crystal Sparkle **have been living** in a large log cabin by a river for five years | Jim and Crystal Sparkle **live** in a large log cabin by a river for five years |

## Possessive forms:

**'Who's' instead of 'whose':**

| Incorrect | Correct |
|---|---|
| The story is about a woman **who's** son has died | The story is about a woman **whose** son has died |

**'It's' instead of 'its':**

| Incorrect | Correct |
|---|---|
| This is an intriguing story, **it's** setting is significant | This is an intriguing story, **its** setting is significant |

**Use of the definite article in possessive forms:**

| Incorrect | Correct |
|---|---|
| The Spielberg film **Spielberg's** film | The Spielberg's film |

## Countable and uncountable nouns

**'informations' instead of 'information':**

| **Incorrect** | **Correct** |
|---|---|
| We are given **much information** about the characters' thoughts | We are given **many informations** about the characters' thoughts |

**'Evidences' instead of 'evidence':**

| **Incorrect** | **Correct** |
|---|---|
| We have **little evidence** that the author is being ironic | We have **few evidences** that the author is being ironic |

## Vocabulary

**'Admit' instead of 'accept':**

| **Incorrect** | **Correct** |
|---|---|
| Her son is dead and she can't **accept** it | Her son is dead and she can't **admit** it |

**'Accept' instead of 'agree':**

| **Incorrect** | **Correct** |
|---|---|

| | |
|---|---|
| He **agreed** to come to the cinema | He **accepted** to come to the cinema |

**'Actual' instead of 'current':**

| **Incorrect** | **Correct** |
|---|---|
| The article is in the **current** edition of *Le Monde Diplomatique* | The article is in the **actual** edition of *Le Monde Diplomatique* |

**'Current' instead of 'common':**

| **Incorrect Sentence** | **Correct Sentence** |
|---|---|
| *The story offers a metaphor for a common misunderstanding between generations* | *The story offers a metaphor for a current misunderstanding between generations* |

**'Good' instead of 'right/correct':**

| **Incorrect Sentence** | **Correct Sentence** |
|---|---|
| *Mrs. Leo tries to take the right/correct decision* | *Mrs. Leo tries to take the good decision* |

**'Good' instead of 'well':**

| **Incorrect Sentence** | **Correct Sentence** |
|---|---|
| *They knew each other really well* | *They knew each other really good* |

**'Good' instead of 'effective':**

| Incorrect Sentence | Correct Sentence |
|---|---|
| *The description of the place is most effective* | *The description of the place is most good* |

**'Loose' instead of 'lose':**

| Incorrect Sentence | Correct Sentence |
|---|---|
| *She does not want to lose her memories of him* | *She does not want to loose her memories of him* |

**'Remember' instead of 'remind':**

| Incorrect Sentence | Correct Sentence |
|---|---|
| *She decides to remove all the things which could remind her of her son* | *She decides to remove all the things which could remember her of her son* |

---

**'Support' instead of 'bear' or 'stand':**

| Incorrect Sentence | Correct Sentence |
|---|---|
| *She does this because she can't bear/stand seeing the door locked* | *She does this because she can't support seeing the door locked* |

**'This' instead of 'it is' (as a translation of 'c'est' at the beginning of sentences):**

| Incorrect Sentence | Correct Sentence |
|---|---|
| *It is here that the story really begins* | *This is here that the story really begins* |

**'According to me' instead of 'in my opinion' (in my view, as I see it, etc.):**

| Incorrect Sentence | Correct Sentence |
|---|---|
| *In my opinion, the title of the story reflects Mrs. Cameron's state of mind* | *According to me, the title of the story reflects Mrs. Cameron's state of mind* |

**'Tell' instead of 'speak':**

| Incorrect Sentence | Correct Sentence |
|---|---|
| *In this story, Kate Chopin speaks about social class* | *In this story, Kate Chopin tells about social class* |

**'Make' instead of 'do':**

| Incorrect Sentence | Correct Sentence |
|---|---|
| *But we don't know what her husband does to her* | *But we don't know what her husband makes her* |

**'Develop' instead of 'analyse':**

| Incorrect Sentence | Correct Sentence |
|---|---|

| | |
|---|---|
| *I will now analyse the symbolism of the house* | *I will now develop the house's symbolism* |

---

**'Remark' instead of 'notice':**

| **Incorrect Sentence** | **Correct Sentence** |
|---|---|
| *He wants to talk to her but then notices that…* | *He wants to talk to her but then remarks that…* |

**'Find again' instead of 'rediscover':**

| **Incorrect Sentence** | **Correct Sentence** |
|---|---|
| *She wants to rediscover the traces of his existence* | *She wants to find again the traces of his existence* |

**'Project' instead of 'plan':**

| **Incorrect Sentence** | **Correct Sentence** |
|---|---|
| *She has to do what she planned* | *She has to do what she projected* |

**'Decease' instead of 'die':**

| **Incorrect Sentence** | **Correct Sentence** |
|---|---|
| *Time stopped when Harry died* | *Time stopped when Harry deceased* |

**'Get in' instead of 'enter':**

| Incorrect Sentence | Correct Sentence |
|---|---|
| *As soon as she enters the house* | *As soon as she gets in the house* |

**'Critic' instead of 'review':**

| Incorrect Sentence | Correct Sentence |
|---|---|
| *I have read a very good review of that book* | *I have read a very good critic of that book* |

**Confusion of noun with adjectival form, e.g. 'ironic' instead of 'irony':**

| Incorrect Sentence | Correct Sentence |
|---|---|
| *The last sentence of the story is ironic* | *The last sentence of the story is irony* |

**Confusion of the noun form with the infinitive, e.g. 'apologies' with 'apologize':**

| Incorrect Sentence | Correct Sentence |
|---|---|
| *I must apologize for being late* | *I must apologies for being late* |

**'News' with 'are' instead of 'is':**

| Incorrect Sentence | Correct Sentence |
|---|---|
| *What is the latest news?* | *What are the latest news?* |

**Failure to capitalize days of the week and adjectives of nationality:**

| **Incorrect Sentence** | **Correct Sentence** |
|---|---|
| *See you on Wednesday* | *See you on wednesday* |
| *His behaviour is classically Nigerian* | *His behaviour is classically nigerian* |

# SEGMENT 4

## Adjectives Examples

Looking at examples of adjectives can make it easier to understand how this important part of speech is used within the English Language.

## Popular Adjectives

An adjective is a word that describes, identifies or further defines a noun or a pronoun. There are thousands of adjectives available to describe how something feels, looks, sounds, tastes and acts. Here are a few examples.

**To Describe Taste**

| | | |
|---|---|---|
| Bitter | Lemon-flavored | Spicy |
| Bland | Minty | Sweet |
| Delicious | Pickled | Tasty |
| Fruity | Salty | Tasty |
| Gingery | Sour | Yummy |

**To Describe Touch**

| | | |
|---|---|---|
| Auricular | Boiling | Fluffy |
| Freezing | Sharp | Silky |
| Breezy | Bumpy | Fuzzy |
| Greasy | Slick | Slimy |
| Chilly | Cold | Hard |
| Hot | Slippery | Smooth |
| Cool | Lev | Soft |

| Cuddly | Damaged | Loose |
|---|---|---|
| Melted | Solid | Steady |
| Damp | Dirty | Painful |
| Plastic | Sticky | Tender |
| Div | Dusty | Filthy |
| Prickly | Rough | Shaggy |
| Tight | Uneven | Warm |
| Flaky | Shaky | Wet |

**To Describe Sound**

| Blaring | Deafening | Melodic |
|---|---|---|
| Moaning | Screeching | Shrill |
| Faint | Hoarse | Muffled |
| Mute | Silent | Soft |
| High-pitched | Hissing | Noisy |
| Purring | Squealing | Squeaking |
| Hushed | Quiet | Thundering |
| Husky | Loud | Raspy |
| Resonant | Voiceless | Whispering |

**To Describe Color**

| Azure | Gray | Pinkish |
|---|---|---|
| Black | Blue | Bright |
| Green | Indigo | Lavender |
| Purple | Red | Rosy |
| Brown | Crimson | Light |
| Magenta | Scarlet | Silver |
| Dark | Drab | Multi-coloured |
| Mustard | Turquoise | Violet |
| Dull | Orange | White |
| Gold | Pink | Yellow |

**To Describe Size**

| | | |
|---|---|---|
| Abundant | Big-boned | Jumbo |
| Large | Puny | Scrawny |
| Chubby | Fat | Giant |
| Little | Long | Majestic |
| Short | Small | Tall |
| Gigantic | Great | Mammoth |
| Massive | Teeny | Thin |
| Huge | Immense | Miniature |
| Petite | Tiny | Vast |

**To Describe Shape**

| | | |
|---|---|---|
| Blobby | Broad | Distorted |
| Flat | Rotund | Round |
| Chubby | Circular | Fluffy |
| Globular | Skinny | Square |
| Crooked | Curved | Hollow |
| Low | Steep | Straight |
| Cylindrical | Narrow | Triangular |
| Deep | Oval | Wide |

**To Describe Time**

| | | |
|---|---|---|
| Annual | Brief | Futuristic |
| Historical | Rapid | Regular |
| Daily | Early | Eternal |
| Irregular | Late | Lone |
| Short | Slow | Speed |
| Fast | First | Modern |
| Old | Speedy | Swift |

| | | |
|---|---|---|
| Fleet | Future | Old-fashioned |
| Quick | Waiting | Young |

**To Describe an Amount**

| | | |
|---|---|---|
| Ample | Several | Few |
| Bountiful | Countless | Little |
| Considerable | Many | Meager |
| Numerous | Multiple | Sparse |
| Plentiful | Some | Teeny |
| Profuse | Sizable | Tiny |
| Substantial | Sufficient | Me |

**To Describe an Emotion**

| | | |
|---|---|---|
| Abrasive | Embarrassed | Grumpy |
| Abrupt | Energetic | Kind |
| Afraid | Enraged | Lazy |
| Agreeable | Enthusiastic | Lively |
| Aggressive | Envious | Lonely |
| Amiable | Evil | Lucky |
| Amused | Excited | Mad |
| Angry | Exhausted | Manic |
| Annoyed | Exuberant | Mysterious |
| Ashamed | Fair | Nervous |
| Bad | Faithful | Obedient |
| Bitter | Fantastic | Obnoxious |
| Bewildered | Fierce | Outrageous |
| Boring | Fine | Panicky |
| Brave | Foolish | Perfect |
| Callous | Frantic | Persuasive |
| Calm | Frightened | Proud |
| Calming | Funny | Quirky |
| Charming | Furious | Relieved |

| Cheerful | Gentle | Repulsive |
|---|---|---|
| Combative | Glib | Rundown |
| Comfortable | Glorious | Sad |
| Defeated | Good | Scary |
| Confused | Grateful | Selfish |
| Cooperative | Grieving | Silly |
| Courageous | Gusty | Splendid |
| Cowardly | Gutsy | Successful |
| Crabby | Happy | Tedious |
| Creepy | Healthy | Tense |
| Cross | Heinous | Terrible |
| Cruel | Helpless | Thankful |
| Dangerous | He In fill | Thoughtful |
| Defeated | Hilarious | Thoughtless |
| Defiant | Homeless | Tired |
| Delightful | Hurt | Troubled |
| Depressed | Hungry | Upset |
| Determined | Immoral | Weak |
| Disgusted | Indignant | Weary |
| Disturbed | Irate | Wicked |
| Eager | Itchy | Worried |
| Elated | Jealous | Zany |
| Embarrassed | Jolly | Zealous |

**To Describe a Person or Personality**

| Aggressive | Famous | Restless |
|---|---|---|
| Agoraphobic | Fearless | Rich |
| Ambidextrous | Fertile | Righteous |
| Ambitious | Fragile | Ritzy |
| Amoral | Frank | Romantic |
| Angelic | Functional | Rustic |
| Brainy | Gabby | Ruthless |
| Careless | Cautious | Stingy |
| Cheerful | Innocent | Inquisitive |

| | | |
|---|---|---|
| Insane | Sleenv | Somber |
| Clever | Common | Jaunty |
| Juicy | Stupid | Sure |
| Complete | Concerned | Macho |
| Manly | Swanky | Tame |
| Crazy | Curious | Dead |
| Modern | Mushy | Naughty |
| Tawdry | Terrific | Testy |
| Deep | Delightful | Odd |
| Old | Uninterested | Vague |
| Determined | Different | Open |
| Outstanding | Verdant | Vivacious |
| Diligent | Energetic | Erratic |
| Perky | Poor | Powerful |
| Wacky | Wandering | Wild |
| Evil | Exuberant | Puzzled |
| Real | Womanly | Wrong |

**To Describe Appearance**

| | | |
|---|---|---|
| Ablaze | Adorable | Distinct |
| Drab | Quirky | Ruddy |
| Alluring | Attractive | Dull |
| Elegant | Shiny | Skinny |
| Average | Awkward | Embarrassed |
| Fancy | Sloppy | Smiling |
| Balanced | Fat | Sparkling |
| Beautiful | Blonde | Filthy |
| Glamorous | Spotless | Strange |
| Bloody | Blushing | Gleaming |
| Flossy | Tacky | Tall |
| Bright | Clean | Clear |
| Graceful | Grotesque | Handsome |
| Thin | Ugly | Unattractive |

| | | |
|---|---|---|
| Cloudy | Clumsy | Homely |
| Interior | Unbecoming | Uncovered |
| Colorful | Confident | Lovely |
| Magnificent | Unsightly | Unusual |
| Cracked | Crooked | Crushed |
| Murky | Old-fashioned | Plain |
| Watery | Weird | Wild |
| Curly | Cute | Poised |
| Pretty | Wiry | Wooden |
| Debonair | Dirty | Puffy |
| Quaint | Worried | Zaftig |

**To Describe Situations**

| | | |
|---|---|---|
| Accidental | Achievable | Doubtful |
| Elementary | Main | Minor |
| Advantageous | Alcoholic | Finger-Printed |
| Groundless | Nasty | Nutritious |
| Animated | Aquatic | Hard |
| Harmful | Obsolete | Optimal |
| Aromatic | High | Organic |
| Aspiring | Bad | Honest |
| Horrible | Premium | Quizzical |
| Bawdy | Biographical | Illegal |
| Illegible | Rainy | Redundant |
| Bizarre | Broken | Careful |
| Imperfect | Impossible | Internal |
| Remarkable | Simple | Tangible |
| Credible | Green | Inventive |
| Jazzy | Tricky | Wholesale |
| Cumbersome | Disastrous | Juvenile |
| Legal | Worse | Wry |
| Dismissive | Logical | X-rated |

## Using Adjectives in Writing

While it is important to understand how adjectives add to the descriptions of the nouns and pronouns, it is also wise to understand how to effectively use adjectives in your own writings.

Adjectives are best used sparingly. Generally, nouns and verbs should do the bulk of the descriptive work in your prose. Don't simply tell your reader that something is beautiful, exciting, or interesting. Use your words to show why these descriptive labels are appropriate.

# SEGMENT 5

## Commonly Misused Words and Phrases

The transition from spoken to written language can often be a bumpy one because the way we talk tends to be a lot less formal than the way we write. When we try to translate spoken ideas into writing, it is often hard to remember correct grammar. Also, we hear incorrect grammar used so often that correct grammar might sound odd or even wrong to us.

Homophones can present an especially difficult problem because they sound alike, but the different spellings mean different things. Changing one letter in a word could alter the whole meaning of a sentence. Common phrases are also likely to be written incorrectly because in speech, words are often shortened or slurred together so that not all of the letters are pronounced, making it easy to inadvertently leave these letters out when writing.

Knowing which word to use or how to write a phrase correctly can make a big difference in your writing. It is easier for readers to take a piece of writing more seriously when the grammar is correct. This segment contains a list of commonly confused homonyms and problem phrases, as well as a few hints to help you remember the grammar rules.

## Words that sound alike (homophones)

**Accept, Except:**

Accept is a verb meaning to receive.
Except is usually a preposition meaning excluding.
*I will accept all the packages except that one.*
Except is also a verb meaning to exclude.
*Please except that item from the list.*

**Affect, Effect:**

Affect is usually a verb meaning to influence.
Effect is usually a noun meaning result.
*The drug did not affect the disease, and it had several adverse side effects.*
Effect can also be a verb meaning to bring about.
*Only the president can effect such a dramatic change.*

**Allusion, Illusion:**

Allusion is an indirect reference.
Illusion is a misconception or false impression.
*Did you catch my allusion to Shakespeare?*
*Mirrors give the room an illusion of depth.*

**Capital, Capitol:**

Capital refers to a city, capitol to a building where lawmakers meet.
Capital also refers to wealth or resources.
*The capitol has undergone extensive renovations.*
*The residents of the state capital protested the development plans.*

**Climactic, Climatic:**

Climactic is derived from climax, the point of greatest intensity in a series or progression of events.
Climatic is derived from climate; it refers to meteorological conditions.
*The climactic period in the dinosaurs' reign was reached just before severe climatic conditions brought on the ice age.*

**Elicit, Illicit:**

Elicit is a verb meaning to bring out or to evoke.
Illicit is an adjective meaning unlawful.
*The reporter was unable to elicit information from the police about illicit drug traffic.*

**Emigrate from, Immigrate to:**

Emigrate means to leave one country or region to settle in another.
*In 1900, my grandfather emigrated from Russia.*
Immigrate means to enter another country and reside there.
*Many Mexicans immigrate to the U.S. to find work.*

**Hints:**

Emigrate begins with the letter **E**, as does **Exit**. When you emigrate, you exit a country.

Immigrate begins with the letter **I**, as does **In**. When you immigrate, you go into a country.

**Principle, Principal:**

Principal is a noun meaning the head of a school or an organization or a sum of money.
Principle is a noun meaning a basic truth or law.
*The principal taught us many important life principles.*

**Hint:**

To recognize the spelling of **Principal**, first think of yourself as a greedy opportunist. You definitely would want to be a **pal** of anyone who is in a position of power or anything to do with money. This **principal** has **pal** in it.

**Than, Then:**

**Than** is a conjunction used in comparisons; **then** is an adverb denoting time.
*That pizza is more than I can eat.*
*Tom laughed, and then we recognized him.*

**Hints:**

**Than** is used to compare; both words have the letter **a** in them.

**Then** tells when; both are spelled the same, except for the first letters.

**There, Their, They're:**

**There** is an adverb specifying place; it is also an expletive.
*Adverb: Sylvia is lying there unconscious.*
*Expletive: There are two plums left.*

**Their** is a possessive pronoun.
**They're** is a contraction of they are.
*Fred and Jane finally washed their car.*
*They're later than usual today.*

**Hints:**

If you are using **there** to tell the reader **where**, both words have **h-e-r-e**.

If you are using **their** as a possessive pronoun, it has **h-e-i-r**, which also means heir, as in someone who inherits something.

**They're** is a contraction of **they are**. Sound out **they are** in the sentence and see if it works. If it does not, it must be one of the previous versions.

**To, Too, Two:**

**To** is a preposition; **too** is an adverb; **two** is a number.
*Too many of your shots slice to the left, but the last two were right on the mark.*

**Hints:**

If you are trying to spell out the number, it is always **t-w-o**.

**Too** is usually used as **also** when adding or including some additional information.

**Your, You're:**

**Your** is a possessive pronoun; **you're** is a contraction of **you are**.
*You're going to catch a cold if you don't wear your coat.*

**Hints:**

Sound out **you are** in the sentence. If it works in the sentence, it can be written as **you're**. If it sounds awkward, it is probably supposed to be **your**.

**Example:**
*You're shoes are muddy.*
**You are shoes are muddy** does not work, so it should be written as:
*Your shoes are muddy.*

## Words that don't sound alike but confuse us anyway

### Lie, Lay:

**Lie** is an intransitive verb meaning to recline or rest on a surface. Its principal parts are **lie, lay, lain**.
**Lay** is a transitive verb meaning to put or place. Its principal parts are **lay, laid**.

**Hint:**
*Chickens lay eggs. I lie down when I am tired.*

### Set, Sit:

**Set** is a transitive verb meaning to put or to place. Its principal parts are **set, set, set**.
**Sit** is an intransitive verb meaning to be seated. Its principal parts are **sit, sat, sat**.
*She set the dough in a warm corner of the kitchen.*
*The cat sat in the warmest part of the room.*

**Who, Which, That:**

Do not use **which** to refer to persons. Use **who** instead. **That**, though generally used to refer to things, may be used to refer to a group or class of people.
*I just saw a boy who was wearing a yellow banana costume.*
*I have to go to math next, which is my hardest class.*
*Where is the book that I was reading?*

## Problem phrases

**Supposed to:** Do not omit the **d**. *Suppose to* is incorrect.

**Used to:** Same as above. Do not write *use to*.

**Toward:** There is no **s** at the end of the word.

**Anyway:** Also has no ending **s**. *Anyways* is nonstandard.

**Couldn't care less:** Be sure to make it negative. (*Not I could care less.*)

**All walks of life:** *Not works of life.* This phrase does not apply to oriental cooking.

**Chest of drawers:** *Not Chester drawers.*

**For all intents and purposes:** *Not intensive purposes.*

---

*Source: A Writer's Reference, Diana Hacker*

# SEGMENT 6

## REGULAR AND IRREGULAR VERBS WE USE

### Regular Verbs: A Vocabulary List

**A**

| | | | | |
|---|---|---|---|---|
| Accept | Adopt | Amuse | Appreciate | Assure |
| Ache | Affirm | Analyze | Approve | Attach |
| Acknowledge | Afford | Announce | Argue | Attack |
| Act | Agree | Annoy | Arrange | Attempt |
| Add | Ail | Answer | Arrest | Attend |
| Admire | Alert | Apologize | Arrive | Attract |
| Admit | Allege | Appeal | Articulate | Auction |
| Admonish | Allude | Appear | Ask | Avoid |
| Advise | Allow | Applaud | Assert | Avow |

**B**

| | | | | |
|---|---|---|---|---|
| Babble | Barrage | Bellow | Boast | Brake |
| Back | Barter | Belong | Bob | Branch |
| Bake | Baste | Berate | Boil | Brand |
| Balance | Bat | Besiege | Bolt | Breathe |
| Balk | Bathe | Bestow | Bomb | Broil |
| Ban | Battle | Bleach | Book | Bruise |
| Bang | Bawl | Bless | Bore | Brush |
| Bandage | Beam | Blind | Borrow | Bubble |
| Bar | Befriend | Blink | Bounce | Bump |
| Bare | Beg | Blot | Bow | Burnish |
| Bargain | Behave | Blurt | Box | Bury |
| Bark | Believe | Blush | Brag | Buzz |

## C

| | | | | | |
|---|---|---|---|---|---|
| Cajole | Chew | Color | Confide | Crack | |
| Calculate | Chide | Comb | Confirm | Crash | |
| Call | Chip | Comfort | Connect | Crave | |
| Camp | Choke | Command | Consent | Crawl | |
| Care | Chomp | Comment | Consider | Crochet | |
| Carry | Chop | Communicate | Consist | Cross | |
| Carve | Claim | Compare | Contain | Criticize | |
| Cause | Clap | Compete | Contend | Croak | |
| Caution | Clean | Complain | Continue | Cross- | |
| Challenge | Clear | Complete | Cook | Examine | |
| Change | Climb | Concede | Copy | Crowd | |
| Chant | Clip | Concentrate | Correct | Crush | |
| Charge | Close | Concern | Cough | Cry | |
| Chase | Coach | Conclude | Count | Cure | |
| Cheat | Coil | Concur | Counter | Curl | |
| Check | Collect | Confess | Cover | Curse | |
| Cheer | Chew | Covet | Cycle | | |

## D

| | | | | |
|---|---|---|---|---|
| Dam | Decorate | Deter | Divulge | Drip |
| Damage | Delay | Develop | Dial | Dictate |
| Die | Digress | Direct | Disclose | Dislike |
| Dive | Divide | Divorce | Dock | Dole |
| Dote | Double | Doubt | Drag | Drain |
| Dress | Drill | Dance | Delight | Drone |
| Dare | Deliver | Drop | Drown | Deal |
| Demand | Debate | Decay | Deny | Depend |
| Dry | Dupe | Deceive | Describe | Dump |
| Decide | Desert | Dust | Decipher | Deserve |
| Dye | Declare | Desire | | |

## E

| | | | | |
|---|---|---|---|---|
| Cam | Emphasize | Enjoy | Echo | Employ |
| Enter | Evaporate | Exaggerate | Expand | Expect |
| Edit | Empty | Entertain | Educate | Enchant |
| Enunciate | Elope | Encode | Envy | Embarrass |
| Encourage | Equivocate | Emigrate | End | Escape |
| Emit | Enjoin | Evacuate | Examine | Excite |
| Excuse | Exercise | Exclaim | Exhort | Exist |
| Expel | Explain | Explode | Explore | Extend |
| Extol | | | | |

## F

| | | | | |
|---|---|---|---|---|
| Lace | Fear | Fish | Floss | Forgive |
| Fade | Fence | Fit | Flow | Form |
| Fail | Fetch | Fix | Flower | Found |
| Falter | File | Flap | Fold | Frame |
| Fasten | Fill | Flash | Follow | Fret |
| Favor | Film | Float | Fool | Frighten |
| Fax | Fire | Flood | Force | Fry |
| Fume | | | | |

## G

| | | | | |
|---|---|---|---|---|
| Garden | Gasp | Gather | Gaze | Gel |
| Gild | Glide | Glue | Gnaw | Grab |
| Grate | Grease | Greet | Grill | Grin |
| Grip | Groan | Growl | Grumble | Grunt |
| Guarantee | Guard | Guess | Guide | Gush |

## I

| | | | | |
|---|---|---|---|---|
| Ice | Identify | Ignore | Imagine | Immigrate |
| Implore | Impress | Improve | Include | Increase |
| Infect | Inflate | Influence | Inform | Infuse |
| Inject | Injure | Inquire | Insist | Inspect |
| Inspire | Instruct | Intend | Interest | Interfere |
| Interject | Interrupt | Introduce | Invent | Invest |
| Invite | Irritate | Iron | Itch | |

## J

| | | | | |
|---|---|---|---|---|
| Jab | Jabber | Jail | Jam | Jeer |
| Jest | Jog | Join | Joke | Jolt |
| Judge | Juggle | Jump | | |

## K

| | | | | |
|---|---|---|---|---|
| Kick | Kill | Kiss | Knock | Knot |

## L

| | | | | |
|---|---|---|---|---|
| Label | Lean | Lift | Listen | Long |
| Lament | Lecture | Lighten | Live | Look |
| Land | Level | Like | Load | Loosen |
| Last | License | List | Loan | Love |
| Laugh | Lick | Lock | Lower | |

# M

| | | | | |
|---|---|---|---|---|
| Mail | Mark | Melt | Mine | Move |
| Maintain | Marry | Memorize | Miss | Mow |
| Man | Marvel | Mend | Mix | Mug |
| Manage | Mate | Mention | Moan | Multiply |
| Mar | Matter | Merge | Moor | Mumble |
| March | Measure | Milk | Mourn | Murder |
| Molt | Mutter | | | |

# N

| | | | | |
|---|---|---|---|---|
| Nag | Name | Need | Nod | Notice |
| Nail | Nap | Nest | Note | Number |

# O

| | | | | |
|---|---|---|---|---|
| Obey | Obtain | Offer | Omit | Overflow |
| Object | Occur | Ogle | Open | Owe |
| Observe | Offend | Oil | Operate | Own |
| Order | | | | |

# P

| | | | | |
|---|---|---|---|---|
| Pack | Peer | Plead | Pray | Produce |
| Pad | Peg | Please | Preach | Profess |
| Paddle | Pelt | Pledge | Precede | Program |
| Paint | Perform | Plow | Predict | Promise |
| Pant | Permit | Plug | Prefer | Propose |
| Park | Pester | Point | Prepare | Protect |
| Part | Pet | Poke | Present | Protest |
| Pass | Phone | Polish | Preserve | Provide |
| Paste | Pick | Ponder | Press | Pry |
| Pat | Pinch | Pop | Pretend | Pull |
| Pause | Pine | Possess | Prevent | Pump |
| Peck | Place | Post | Prick | Punch |
| Pedal | Plan | Postulate | Print | Puncture |
| Peel | Plant | Pour | Proceed | Punish |
| Play | Practice | Proclaim | Push | |

# Q

| | | | |
|---|---|---|---|
| Question | Quilt | Quiz | Quote |

## R

| Race | Radiate | Rain | Raise | Rant |
|---|---|---|---|---|
| Rate | Receive | Recite | Recognize | Recommend |
| Record | Reduce | Reflect | Rejoice | Relate |
| Relax | Release | Rely | Remain | Remember |
| Reply | Report | Reprimand | Reproduce | Request |
| Rescue | Retire | Rinse | Risk | Roar |
| Rob | Rock | Roll | Rot | Rave |
| Reach | Realize | Rebuff | Recall | Refuse |
| Regret | Reign | Reiterate | Reject | Remind |
| Remove | Repair | Repeat | Replace | Retort |
| Return | Reveal | Reverse | Rhyme | Row |
| Rub | Run | Rule | Rush | |

## S

| Sack | Sail | Settle | Sever | Ski |
|---|---|---|---|---|
| Skip | Soak | Sob | Stare | Start |
| Strut | Stun | Satisfy | Save | Savor |
| Saw | Scare | Scatter | Scoff | Scold |
| Scoot | Scorch | Scrape | Shade | Shampoo |
| Share | Shave | Shelter | Shift | Shiver |
| Shock | Shop | Shout | Shriek | Slap |
| Slice | Slip | Slow | Smash | Smell |
| Smile | Smoke | Snap | Snarl | Snatch |
| Soothe | Sound | Span | Spare | Spark |
| Sparkle | Speculate | Spell | Spill | Spoil |
| Spot | Spray | Sprout | Sputter | Squash |
| Squeeze | Stab | Stain | Stammer | Stamp |
| Star | Stash | State | Stay | Steer |
| Step | Stipulate | Stir | Stitch | Stop |
| Store | Strap | Storm | Stow | Strengthen |
| Stress | Stretch | Strip | Stroke | Stuff |
| Stray | Strum | Stunt | Stutter | Submerge |
| Succeed | Suffer | Suggest | Suit | Supply |
| Support | Suppose | Surmise | Surprise | Surround |
| Suspect | Suspend | Sway | Swear | Swing |
| Switch | Swoop | Sympathize | Scratch | Scream |
| Shrug | Sigh | Sneak | Sneer | Screech |
| Screw | Sign | Signal | Sneeze | Snicker |
| Scribble | Seal | Search | Sense | Separate |
| Serve | Sin | Singe | Sip | Skate |
| Skateboard | Sketch | Sniff | Snore | Snoop |
| Snooze | Snort | Snow | | |

## T

| | | | | |
|---|---|---|---|---|
| Talk | Thank | Tire | Translate | Trot |
| Tame | Thaw | Toast | Transport | Trap |
| Travel | Treat | Tremble | Trick | Trickle |
| Trim | Trip | Trouble | Trust | Trounce |
| Try | Tug | Tumble | Turn | Twist |
| Type | Tap | Theorize | Toss | Taste |
| Threaten | Touch | Taunt | Thunder | Tour |
| Tease | Tick | Tow | Telephone | Tickle |
| Trace | Tempt | Tie | Track | Terrify |
| Time | Trade | Testify | Tip | Train |

## V

| | | | | | |
|---|---|---|---|---|---|
| Vacuum | Value | Vanish | Vanquish | Venture | |
| Visit | | | | | |

## W

| | | | | | |
|---|---|---|---|---|---|
| Voice | Volunteer | Vote | Vouch | Wail | |
| Warn | Wed | Whisper | Work | Wait | |
| Wash | Weigh | Whistle | Worry | Walk | |
| Waste | Welcome | Wink | Wrap | Wallow | |
| Watch | Whimper | Wipe | Wreck | Wander | |
| Water | Whine | Wish | Wrestle | Want | |
| Wave | Whip | Wobble | Wriggle | Warm | |
| Waver | Whirl | Wonder | Writhe | | |

| **X** | **Y** | **Z** |
|---|---|---|
| X-Ray | Yawn | Zip |
| | Yell | Zoom |
| | Yelp | |
| | Yield | |
| | Yodel | |

## A

| | |
|---|---|
| Arise (Arose, Arisen) | Awake (Awoke, Awoken) |

## B

| | | |
|---|---|---|
| Be (Was/Were, Been) | Bet (Bet, Bet) | Breed (Bred, Bred) |
| Bear (Bore, Born/Borne) | Bind (Bound, Bound) | Bring (Brought, Brought) |
| Beat (Beat, Beaten) | Bite (Bit, Bitten) | Build (Built, Built) |

| | | |
|---|---|---|
| Become (Became, Become) | Bleed (Bled, Bled) | Burn (Burned/Burnt, Burned/Burnt) |
| Begin (Began, Begun) | Blow (Blew, Blown) | Burst (Burst, Burst) |
| Bend (Bent, Bent) | Break (Broke, Broken) | Buy (Bought, Bought) |

## C

| | | |
|---|---|---|
| Cast (Cast, Cast) | Cling (Clung, Clung) | Creep (Crept, Crept) |
| Catch (Caught, Caught) | Come (Came, Come) | Cut (Cut, Cut) |
| Choose (Chose, Chosen) | Cost (Cost, Cost) | |

## D

| | | |
|---|---|---|
| Deal (Dealt, Dealt) | Dig (Dug, Dug) | Do (Did, Done) |
| Draw (Drew, Drawn) | Dream (Dreamed/Dreamt, Dreamed/Dreamt) | Drive (Drove, Driven) |
| Drink (Drank, Drunk) | | |

## F

| | | |
|---|---|---|
| Fall (Fell, Fallen) | Feed (Fed, Fed) | Feel (Felt, Felt) |
| Fight (Fought, Fought) | Find (Found, Found) | Flee (Fled, Fled) |
| Fling (Flung, Flung) | Fly (Flew, Flown) | Forbid (Forbade, Forbidden) |
| Forecast (Forecast, Forecast) | Freeze (Froze, Frozen) | |

## G

| | | |
|---|---|---|
| Get (Got, Gotten) | Give (Gave, Given) | Grow (Grew, Grown) |
| Go (Went, Gone) | Grind (Ground, Ground) | |

## H

| | | |
|---|---|---|
| Handwrite (Handwrote, Handwritten) | Hang (Hung, Hung) | Have (Had, Had) |
| Hear (Heard, Heard) | Hide (Hid, Hidden) | Hit (Hit, Hit) |
| Foresee (Foresaw, Foreseen) | Foretell (Foretold, Foretold) | Forget (Forgot, Forgotten) |
| Forgive (Forgave, Forgiven) | Freeze (Froze, Frozen) | Hold (Held, Held) |
| Hurt (Hurt, Hurt) | | |

## I

| | | |
|---|---|---|
| Inbreed (Inbred, Inbred) | Inlay (Inlaid, Inlaid) | Interweave (Interwove, Interwoven) |

## K

| | | |
|---|---|---|
| Keep (Kept, Kept) | Kneel (Knelt/Kneeled, Knelt/Kneeled) | Know (Knew, Known) |

## L

| | | |
|---|---|---|
| Lay (Laid, Laid) | Lead (Led, Led) | Learn (Learned/Learnt, Learned/Learnt) |
| Leave (Left, Left) | Lend (Lent, Lent) | Let (Let, Let) |
| Lie (Lay, Lain) | Lose (Lost, Lost) | |

## M

| | |
|---|---|
| Mean (Meant, Meant) | Meet (Met, Met) |
| Mistake (Mistook, Mistaken) | Misunderstand (Misunderstood, Misunderstood) |

## O

| | | |
|---|---|---|
| Offset (Offset, Offset) | Outbid (Outbid, Outbid) | Outdo (Outdid, Outdone) |
| Outgrow (Outgrew, Outgrown) | Outrun (Outran, Outrun) | Overdo (Overdid, Overdone) |
| Overeat (Overate, Overeaten) | Overhear (Overheard, Overheard) | Oversee (Oversaw, Overseen) |
| Overspend (Overspent, Overspent) | Overtake (Overtook, Overtaken) | Overthrow (Overthrew, Overthrown) |

## P

| | |
|---|---|
| Partake (Partook, Partaken) | Pay (Paid, Paid) |
| Prove (Proved, Proven/Proved) | Put (Put, Put) |

## Q

| | |
|---|---|
| Quit (Quit, Quit) | |

## R

| | | |
|---|---|---|
| Ring (Rang, Rung) | Rise (Rose, Risen) | Run (Ran, Run) |
| Read (Read, Read) | Rid (Rid, Rid) | Ride (Rode, Ridden) |

## S

| | | |
|---|---|---|
| Say (Said, Said) | See (Saw, Seen) | Seek (Sought, Sought) |
| Sell (Sold, Sold) | Send (Sent, Sent) | Set (Set, Set) |
| Sew (Sewed, Sewed/Sewn) | Shake (Shook, Shaken) | Shed (Shed, Shed) |
| Shoot (Shot, Shot) | Show (Showed, Showed/Shown) | Shrink (Shrank, Shrunk) |
| Shut (Shut, Shut) | Sing (Sang, Sung) | Sit (Sat, Sat) |
| Sleep (Slept, Slept) | Slide (Slid, Slid) | Sling (Slung, Slung) |
| Slit (Slit, Slit) | Speak (Spoke, Spoken) | Spend (Spent, Spent) |
| Spin (Spun, Spun) | Spread (Spread, Spread) | Spring (Sprang/Sprung, Sprung) |
| Stand (Stood, Stood) | Stick (Stuck, Stuck) | Sting (Stung, Stung) |
| Stride (Strode, Stridden) | Swear (Swore, Sworn) | Sweep (Swept, Swept) |
| Swim (Swam, Swum) | Swing (Swung, Swung) | |

## T

| | | |
|---|---|---|
| Take (Took, Taken) | Teach (Taught, Taught) | Tear (Tore, Torn) |
| Tell (Told, Told) | Think (Thought, Thought) | Throw (Threw, Thrown) |
| Thrust (Thrust, Thrust) | Tread (Trod, Trodden/Trod) | |

## U

| | |
|---|---|
| Understand (Understood, Understood) | Undo (Undid, Undone) |
| Uphold (Upheld, Upheld) | Upset (Upset, Upset) |

## W

| | | |
|---|---|---|
| Wake (Woke, Woken) | Waylay (Waylaid, Waylaid) | Wear (Wore, Worn) |
| Weave (Wove/Weaved, Woven/Weaved) | Weep (Wept, Wept) | Wet (Wet, Wet) |
| Win (Won, Won) | Wind (Wound, Wound) | Withdraw (Withdrew, Withdrawn) |
| Withhold (Withheld, Withheld) | Wring (Wrung, Wrung) | Write (Wrote, Written) |

# SEGMENT 7

## OTHER WAYS YOU CAN RENDER CERTAIN WORDS OR PHRASES

### Descriptive Words

| **LARGE** | **FAST** | **SAID** | **HARD** | **WALK** |
|---|---|---|---|---|
| Big | Accelerated | Asked | Challenging | Hike |
| Colossal | Active | Called | Complicated | March |
| Enormous | Agile | Responded | Demanding | Pace |
| Gigantic | Brisk | Stated | Grueling | Saunter |
| Huge | Rapid | Told | Puzzling | Shuffle |
| Massive | Quick | Commented | Rigid | Stroll |
| Substantial | Speedy | Replied | Tough | Strut |
| Tremendous | Swift | Remarked | Tricky | Wander |

| **HAPPY** | **KIND** | **SAID (cont.)** | **HARD (cont.)** | **WALK (cont.)** |
|---|---|---|---|---|
| Blissful | Benevolent | Declared | Rugged | Jog |
| Cheerful | Considerate | Exclaimed | Sad | Race |
| Delighted | Courteous | Shouted | Dejected | Rush |
| Elate | Helpful | Whispered | Depressed | Scurry |
| Glad | Loving | Announced | Disheartened | |
| Jolly | Patient | Boasted | Forlorn | |
| Jovial | Sweet | Explained | Gloomy | |
| Joyful | Thoughtful | | Glum | |

| HAPPY (cont.) | KIND (cont.) | SMALL |
|---|---|---|
| Amusing | Easy | Diminutive |
| Funny | Apparent | Little |
| Comical | Carefree | Miniature |
| Entertaining | Effortless | Tiny |
| Gleeful | Manageable | Petite |
| Hilarious | Obvious | Teeny |
| Humorous | Simply | Wee |
| Whimsical | Snap | Run |
| Witty | Uncomplicated | Dart |

| HAPPY | UPSET | KIND | GREAT | BAD |
|---|---|---|---|---|
| Cheerful | Down at heart | Amicable | Excellent | Awful |
| Delightful | Miserable | Amiable | Amazing | Appalling |
| Pleased | Frustrated | Courteous | Sensational | Rotten |
| Ecstatic | Distraught | Likeable | Marvelous | Mean |
| Content | Downcast | Gracious | Terrific | Terrible |
| Amused | On edge | Considerate | Splendid | Dreadful |
| Thrilled | Gloomy | Agreeable | Outstanding | Nasty |
| Elated | Despondent | Congenial | Fantastic | Wicked |
| On cloud 9 | Distressed | Approachable | Exceptional | Disagreeable |
| In the 7th heaven | Devastated | Charming | Legendary | Wretched |
| Walking on air | Dispirited | Cute | Awesome | Lousy |

| PRETTY | SCARED | ANGRY | BIG | DIFFICULT |
|---|---|---|---|---|
| Gorgeous | Spooked | Irate | Huge | Thorny |
| Stunning | Agitated | Annoyed | Large | Acute |
| Exquisite | Tense | Touchy | Massive | Pressing |
| Handsome | Apprehensive | Mad | Giant | Hot-button |
| Sensational | Horrified | Cross | Handy | Flabbergasted |
| Appealing | Edgy | Resentful | Enormous | Deep-seated |
| Delicious | Alarmed | Indignant | Tremendous | Puzzling |
| Out of this world | Afraid | Furious | Bulky | Challenging |
| Attractive | Shaken | Infuriated | Hefty | Tricky |
| Mesmerizing | Scared | Seething | Colossal | Bogging |
| Beautiful | Startled | | Immense | Complex |

| INTERESTING | USEFUL | SHOCKED | SMALL | SLANG THAT COMES |
|---|---|---|---|---|
| Exciting | Handy | Taken aback | Tiny | Let it go! |
| Captivating | Practical | Lost for words | Petite | Drop dead! |
| Engaging | | Tongue tight | Minute | Mini touch |
| Thrilling | | Flabbergasted | Minuscule | Freak out! |

| | | | | |
|---|---|---|---|---|
| Gripping | | Staggered | Itsy-bitsy | Don't sweat it! |
| Fascinating | | Shocked | Miniature | Don't blow it! |
| Ripping | | Outraged | Microscopic | Neat |
| Interesting | | Astounded | Skeletal | Don't push it! |
| Astonished | Wee | Give me a break! | | |
| Appalled | | Douche bag | | |

| **SAD** | **HAPPY** | **LIKE** | **LAUGHED** | **RAN** |
|---|---|---|---|---|
| Depressed | Cheerful | Admire | Giggled | Bolted |
| Gloomy | Delightful | Approve | Chuckled | Sped |
| Miserable | Pleased | Adore | Roared | Hurried |
| Cheerless | Glad | Treasure | Howled | Sprinted |
| Unhappy | Joyful | Fancy | Whooped | Jogged |
| Dejected | Ecstatic | Marvel | Snickered | Rushed |
| Forlorn | Content | Respect | Guffawed | Galloped |
| Sorrowful | Jovial | Cherish | Shrieked | Hustled |
| Upset | Amused | | Grinned | Skipped |
| Downcast | Merry | | Cackled | Raced |
| Tearful | Thrilled | | Bellowed | Dashed |
| Somber | Elated | | Chortled | Fled |

| **WALKED** | **LOOKED** |
|---|---|
| Strolled | Looked |
| Sauntered | Gazed |
| Tiptoed | Examined |
| Trotted | Glanced |
| Marched | Viewed |
| Glided | Observed |
| Strutted | Pecked |
| Shuffled | Stared |
| Crept | Watched |
| Trudged | Inspected |
| Hiked | Spied |
| Paraded | Studied |
| Noticed | |

# SEGMENT 8

## IMPLICATIONS OF SEMANTICS

***Improving the understanding of lexical definitions.***

### UNDERSTANDING SEMANTICS:

*Semantics*, derived from the Ancient Greek word *"σημαντικός sēmantikós,"* meaning significant, is the study of meaning or word meanings. It delves into the relationship between signifiers like words, phrases, signs, and symbols, and what they represent, known as their *denotation*.

Improving the understanding of lexical definitions is crucial in various fields, including linguistics, psychology, and computer science. The implications of semantics go beyond mere word meanings. It helps us understand how language works in communication, how we interpret and infer meaning from context, and how we construct meaning through our experiences.

In linguistics, semantics plays a vital role in analyzing language structure and meaning. It helps identify the relationships between words and their meanings, which is essential for natural language processing (NLP) systems used in machine learning and artificial intelligence.

In psychology, semantics is used to study how people understand and process language. It helps us understand how people make sense of words and sentences based on their experiences, knowledge, and context. This knowledge can be applied to improve communication skills or develop language-based therapies for individuals with language disorders.

In computer science, semantics is critical for developing algorithms that can analyze text data accurately. These algorithms can help machines understand human language better and provide more relevant search results or automated translations.

Overall, improving our understanding of semantics has far-reaching implications across various fields. As we continue to explore the relationship between words and their meanings, we can enhance our ability to communicate effectively with others while also advancing technology's capabilities in natural language processing.

## IMPLICATIONS OF SEMANTICS:

The study of semantics has significant implications for various fields, including linguistics, psychology, philosophy, and computer science. By improving our understanding of lexical definitions, we can better comprehend how language works and how it influences our thoughts and behaviors.

One implication is that semantics can help us identify and analyze the meanings of words in different contexts. For example, the same word may have different meanings depending on the context in which it is used. Understanding these nuances can improve communication and prevent misunderstandings.

Another implication is that semantics can aid in language acquisition and development. By studying how words are used and their meanings, we can better understand how to teach them to others. This knowledge can also be applied to natural language processing in computers, allowing them to better understand human language.

Overall, the implications of semantics are far-reaching and have practical applications in many areas of study.

## LINGUISTIC SEMANTICS:

This branch focuses on understanding human expression through language. However, semantics extends beyond linguistics and includes programming languages, formal logics, and semiotics. In scientific circles, semantics is also referred to as *semasiology*.

## SEMANTICS IN CONTEXT:

The term *"semantics"* encompasses a broad spectrum of ideas, ranging from common usage to technical jargon. It often addresses issues related to word selection or connotation in everyday language. Formal semantics has been the subject of extensive inquiry, particularly in linguistics, where it explores the interpretation of signs or symbols within specific circumstances and contexts.

## INTERDISCIPLINARY CONNECTIONS:

The study of semantics intersects with various disciplines, including lexicology, syntax, pragmatics, etymology, and more. It is not only a component of linguistics but also an independent field with its own synthetic properties. Semantics is closely intertwined with the philosophy of language, reference theory, and communication studies, among others.

## SEMANTICS VS. SYNTAX AND PRAGMATICS:

Semantics is distinct from syntax, which focuses on language structure without considering meaning, and pragmatics, which explores the relationship between language symbols, their meaning, and users. Semantics also encompasses representational theories of meaning, such as truth, coherence, and correspondence theories, which are integral to philosophical inquiries into reality and meaning representation.

## SEMANTICS IN LINGUISTICS:

Within linguistics, semantics examines meaning across various linguistic units, including words, phrases, sentences, and larger discourse units. It investigates how meaning attaches to linguistic signs and explores relationships between different units, such as homonymy, synonymy, antonymy, and hypernymy. Additionally, semantics delves into discourse analysis and the connection between meaning and syntax.

## MONTAGUE GRAMMAR:

Richard Montague proposed a semantic system based on *lambda calculus*, which decomposes sentence meaning into parts and combines them using logical predicates. Despite its elegance, Montague grammar faced limitations due to context-dependent word senses, leading to the development of situation semantics and generative lexicon approaches.

## DYNAMIC TURN IN SEMANTICS:

Chomskyan linguistics initially viewed semantic relations as innate, without mechanisms for learning. However, this view could not address issues like metaphor, semantic change, or how perceptual cues are combined in thought. The dynamic turn in semantics seeks to address these shortcomings, emphasizing context-dependent truth values and incomplete semantic categories.

*Semantics* stands as a testament to the boundless depths of human expression. From the nuances of everyday conversation to the intricacies of formal logic, semantics offers a window into the soul of language. As we journey through the ever-expanding universe of meaning, let us embrace the richness of semantics, for it is through understanding that we truly connect.

# SEGMENT 9: LEGAL ENGLISH

## LAW CONCEPTS AND MEANINGS

## LEGAL VOCABULARY 1

| | |
|---|---|
| Arrest (verb) | defend |
| Arrest (noun) | defendant |
| Accuse | defense |
| Acquit | district attorney |
| Adjourn | divorce (noun) |
| Adoption | divorce (verb) |
| Alibi | evidence |
| Alimony | felon |
| Appeal (noun) | felony |
| Appeal (verb) | fine (noun) |
| Arrest (verb) | fine (verb) |
| Attorney | fraud |
| Bankrupt (adjective) | guardian |
| Bribe (noun) | guilty |
| Bribe (verb) | illegal |
| Brief | indict |
| Case | indictment |
| Common law | inmate |
| Contract | intellectual property |
| Copyright (noun) | judge |
| Copyright (verb) | jurisdiction |

| | |
|---|---|
| Court | juror |
| Custody | Justice |
| DA | Landlord |
| Damages (plural) | Lawyer |
| Death sentence | Legal |
| Mediation | Life sentence |
| Negligent | Negligence |
| Notary public | Oath |
| Patent (verb) | Plea |
| Plea bargaining | Power of attorney |
| Prison | Prisoner |
| Probation | Probation officer |
| Property | Prosecute |
| Prosecutor | Restraining order |
| Sentence (noun) | Sentence (verb) |
| Statute | Sue |
| Tenant | Testify |
| Testimony | Trial |
| Verdict | Will |
| Witness (noun) | Witness (verb) |
| Witness stand | |

## COMMON LEGAL TERMS

- **AKA**: *"Also known as"*. Used to list aliases or another name, or another spelling of a name used by a person.
- **Accelerated Rehabilitation**: *Also called AR.* A program that gives persons charged with a crime or motor vehicle violation

for the first time a second chance. The person is placed on probation for up to the charges are dismissed.

- **Acknowledgement**: The signature of a clerk or attorney certifying that the persons filling the document has sworn that the contents are true, and/or that the document is signed by his or her free act and deed.
- **Action**: Also called a case or lawsuit. A civil judicial proceeding where one party sues another for a wrong done, or to protect a right or to prevent a wrong.
- **Adjournment**: Postponement of a court session until another time or place.
- **Adjudication**: A decision or sentence imposed by a judge.
- **Adjudicatory Hearing**: Juvenile court proceeding to determine whether the allegations made in a petition are true and whether the child/youth should be subject to orders of the court.
- **Adult Court Transfer**: The transfer of juveniles who are at least fourteen years old to regular criminal dockets in Geographical Area or Judicial District courts. Also involves the transfer from a Juvenile Detention center to the State Department of Correction.
- **Adult Probation**: A legal status, applied to people 16 years of age and older, who have been convicted of a crime placed under the supervision of a probation officer for a period of time set by the court.

- **Affirmation**: Declaring something to be true under the penalty of perjury by a person who will not take an oath for religious or other reasons.
- **Affidavit**: A written statement made under oath.
- **Alcohol Education Program**: A pre-trial program for the first-time offenders charged with driving a motor vehicle under the influence of alcohol.
- **Alford Doctrine**: A plea in a criminal case in which the defendant does not admit guilt, but agrees that the state has enough evidence against him or her to get a conviction. Allows the defendant to enter into a plea bargain with the State. If the judge accepts to allow plea, a guilty finding is made on the record.
- **Alimony**: Money a court requires one spouse to pay the other spouse for support before and/or after the divorce is granted. If you do not ask for alimony at the final hearing, you can never get it in the future.
- **Allegation**: Saying that something is the assertion, declaration or statement of a party in a case, made in a pleading.
- **Alternate Juror**: A juror selected as a substitute in case another juror must leave the jury panel.
- **Alternative Detention Program**: Programs operated by service providers under the office of Alternative Sanctions used to detain juveniles instead of in a Juvenile Detention Center.
- **Alternative Dispute Resolution**: Also called ADR. Any method used to resolve disputes other than traditional trial

proceedings. For example, mediation. ADR programs speed up the disposition of civil cases.

- **Alternative Incarceration Center**: Also called AIC. A community-based program that provides monitoring, supervision and services to people who would otherwise be incarcerated.
- **Alternative Sanctions**: Criminal punishment that is less restrictive than incarceration.
- **Amicus Curiae brief**: A Latin term meaning "friend of the court." An Amicus Curiae brief is filed by someone who is not a party to a case but has an interest in its outcome. A person who wants to file an amicus curiae brief usually has to get the court's permission to do so.
- **Annulment**: A court order declaring that a marriage is invalid.
- **Answer**: A court document, or pleading, in a civil case, by which the defendant responds to the plaintiff's complaint.
- **Appeal Bond**: Money paid to the court while taking an appeal to cover costs and damages to the other party if the appeal is not successful.
- **Appearance**: The official court form filed with the court clerk which tells the court that you are representing yourself in a lawsuit or criminal case or that an attorney is representing you. All court notices and calendars will be mailed to the address listed on the form. When a defendant in a civil case files an appearance, the person is submitting to the court's jurisdiction.

- **Appellant**: The party appealing a decision or judgment to a higher court.
- **Appellee**: The party against whom an appeal is taken.
- **Arbitration**: Submitting a case or dispute to designated parties for a decision, instead of using a judge.
- **Arraignment**: The first court appearance of a person accused of a crime. The person is advised of his or her rights by a judge and may respond to the criminal charges by entering a plea. Usually happens the morning after a person is arrested.
- **Arrest**: When a person is taken into custody by a police officer and charged with a crime.
- **Arrearages**: Money for alimony and/or child support, which is overdue and unpaid.

• **Assignment List:** A printed list of cases to be presented to the court for hearing.

• **Attachment:** Alien on property or assets to hold it to pay or satisfy any final judgment.

• **Attorney of Record:** Attorney whose name appears in the permanent records or files of a case.

• **Automatic Orders:** Court orders that take effect when a divorce or custody case is started.

• **Bail:** Also called Bond. Money or property given to the court for the temporary release of a defendant, to ensure that the defendant will return to court.

• **Bail Bonds Person:** A person who lends money to a defendant to pay for bail.

• **Bail Commissioner:** A state-appointed person who may set the amount of bond for persons detained at a police station prior to arraignment in court, and who recommends to the court the amount of bond that should be set for the defendant on each criminal case.

• **Bar:** Refers to attorneys as a group.

• **Best Interest of the Child:** The standard a judge uses to decide custody and visitation issues.

• **Bench Warrant:** Court papers issued by the judge, "from the bench," for the arrest of a person.

• **Bond:** Also called bail. Money or property given to the court for the temporary release of a defendant, to ensure that the defendant will return to court. There are two kinds of bonds:

**Non-financial bonds:** a) Non-surety bond where the defendant's signature alone guarantees the amount of bond and the defendant is not required to post any property or retain the services of a professional bail bondsperson as collateral. b) Promise to appear.

**Surety Bond:** The court requires cash, real estate, or a professional bail bond person's signature as collateral before releasing the defendant back into the community. (The court may allow the defendant to post ten percent of the bond in cash to secure his or her release).

• **Bond Forfeiture (Calling the Bond):** If the defendant fails to appear in court as scheduled, the judge may order the bond forfeited (Paid to the state) and the defendant rearrested.

• **Bond Review:** A hearing for a judge to decide if the defendant's bond amount needs to be changed.

• **Bondsman:** A surety; one who has put up cash or property as collateral before a defendant may be released.

• **Brief:** A written document prepared by a lawyer or party on each side of a dispute and filed with the court in support of their arguments.

• **Broken Down Irretrievably:** The most common reason for granting a divorce. It means there is no hope of the husband and wife getting back together again. Also known as "no-fault" divorce.

• **Calendar:** A list of court cases scheduled for a specific date and time; the civil and family court.

• **Calendar Call:** The calling of cases scheduled for the day, usually done at the beginning of each court day.

• **Capital Felony:** A criminal offense in which the death penalty may be imposed (C.G.S. '53A-54B).

• **Case:** A lawsuit or action in a court.

• **Case Conference:** A meeting scheduled by the court to review the case.

• **Case File:** The court file containing papers submitted in a case.

• **Case Flow Coordinator:** A person who keeps track of your case and supervises the scheduling of hearings and trials.

• **Central Transportation Unit:** Persons in the Division of Juvenile Detention Services who provide safe and secure transportation services for juveniles detained at Juvenile Detention Centers, Alternative Detention Program, and Girls' Detention Program.

• **Certify:** To testify in writing; to make known or establish as a fact.

• **CGS:** Abbreviation for Connecticut General Statutes.

• **Challenge:** Rejecting a potential juror.

• **Charge:** Formal accusation of a crime.

• **Charge to Jury:** In trial practice, an address delivered by the court to the jury at the close of the case instructing the jury as to what principles of law they are to apply in reaching a decision.

• **Chattel:** All property except real property, personal property. For example: jewelry, clothing, furniture, and appliances.

• **Child:** Any person under the age of sixteen (16) years of age.

• **Child Support:** Money paid by a parent to help meet the financial needs of a child.

• **The "Chip Smith Charge":** An instruction to deadlocked jurors in civil and criminal cases, urging those jurors who disagree with the majority vote to reexamine the majority views in an effort to reach a unanimous verdict.

• **CIP:** Children in Placement - a voluntary program in Juvenile Court, which monitors neglect cases.

• **Civil Action:** A lawsuit other than a criminal case usually filed in a Judicial District courthouse. This includes family actions (divorces, child support, etc.) and small claims cases, although these are both separately designated.

• **Claim:** In civil cases, the statement of relief desired.

• **Classification and Program Officer (CPO):** A person who provides classification, program, counseling, and recreational services to detained juveniles. May attend certain court hearings in Juvenile Matters and provide reports.

**Common Law:** Laws that develop through case decisions by judges. Not enacted by legislative bodies.

• **Community Service:** Work that convicted defendants are required to perform to repay the community for the harm caused by the crime.

• **Community Services Coordinator:** The person who refers a defendant to community service work and supervises the defendant's completion of that work.

• **Community Service Labor Program:** Also called CSLP. A community service program for persons charged with drug offenses. Upon successful completion of the community service sentence, the criminal case is dismissed.

• **Complaint:** A legal document that tells the court what you want and is served with a summons on the defendant to begin the case.

• **Complex Litigation:** A specialized docket designed for complex civil cases, where one judge hears the case from beginning to end. Criteria include: multiple parties, large amounts of money, lengthy trial, or complex legal issues.

• **Conditional Discharge:** A disposition in criminal cases where the defendant must satisfy certain court-ordered conditions instead of a prison term.

• **Contempt of Court:** A finding that someone disobeyed a court order. Can also mean disrupting court, for example, by being loud or disrespectful to the court.

• **Continuance Date:** Date on which the case will next be heard in court.

• **Contract:** A legally enforceable agreement between two or more persons or parties.

• **Conviction:** To be found guilty of committing a crime.

• **Costs:** Expenses in prosecuting or defending a case in court. Usually does not include attorney's fees.

• **Count:** The different parts of a complaint, which could each be a basis or grounds for the lawsuit.

• **Counter Claim:** A claim by the defendant in a civil action that the defendant is entitled to damages or other relief from the plaintiff.

• **Court-Appointed Attorney:** An attorney who is asked by the court (judge) to either represent a party to the case or to serve in some other capacity that the case requires.

• **Court Clerk:** The person who maintains the official court record of your case. The court clerk's office receives all court papers and assigns hearing dates.

• **Court Interpreter:** The person who translates court hearings from English to another language. Provided at state expense in all criminal cases and in cases enforcing child support orders, if requested. No interpreter is available for divorce or any other civil case.

• **Court Monitor:** The person who prepares a written record of the court hearing for a fee, if requested, from audiotapes made during the hearing.

• **Court Reporter:** The person who records everything said during the court hearing on a stenograph machine and prepares a written record for a fee, if requested.

• **Court Services Officer:** A person who assists the judge and oversees cases as they go through the court.

• **Court Trial:** Trial by a judge, rather than by a jury.

• **Crime Victim Compensation Program:** Awards money to crime victims and their families for medical, mental health, dental, funeral expenses, lost wages, and loss of support.

• **Cross-Examination:** Questioning by a party or the attorney of an adverse party or a witness.

• **Custody:** A court order deciding where a child will live and how decisions about the child will be made. Parents may ask for any custody arrangement they believe is in the interest of their child.

• **Custody Affidavit:** A sworn statement containing facts about a child involved in a case, including the full name of the child, date of birth, current and past residences, and other information as may be required by law.

• **Damages:** Money a party receives as compensation for a legal wrong.

• **Day Incarceration Center:** Also called DIC. A community-based program that provides monitoring, supervision, and services to people who would otherwise be incarcerated. Day Incarceration Center clients are supervised during the daytime hours.

• **Declaration:** An unsworn statement of facts made by a party to the transaction, or by one who has an interest in the facts recounted.

• **Default:** To fail to respond or answer to the plaintiff's claims by filing the required court document; usually an Appearance or an Answer.

• **Defendant:** In civil or family cases, failing to pay an amount of money when due. In juvenile cases, a child who violated a law, local ordinance, or an order of the Superior Court.

• **Deposition:** Testimony of a witness taken under oath in response to another party's questions. Testimony is given outside the courtroom, usually in a lawyer's office. A word-for-word account (transcript) is made of the testimony.

• **Detention Hearing or Detention Release Hearing:** A hearing on the first business day after a juvenile is admitted to juvenile detention concerning the legality and appropriateness of continued detention of the juvenile. The detention decision must be reviewed at least every fifteen days.

- **Discovery:** A formal request by one party in a lawsuit to disclose information or facts known by other parties or witnesses.

- **Dismissal**: A judge's decision to end the case.

- **Dismissal without Prejudice:** A judge's decision to end the case which permits the complainant or prosecutor to renew the case later. In contrast, dismissal "with prejudice" prevents the complainant or prosecutor to bring or maintain the same claim or action again.

- **Dispose**: Ending a legal case or a judicial proceeding.

- **Disposition**: The manner in which a case is settled or resolved.

- **Dissolution**: The legal end of a marriage, also called divorce.

- **Diversionary Programs:** Community based programs that are used to keep eligible, convicted criminal offenders out of prison.

- **Docket**: A list of cases scheduled to be heard in court on a specific day or week.

- **Docket Number:** A unique number the court clerk assigns to a case. It must be used on all future papers filed in the court case. Each docket number starts with two letters that tell the type of case. CI = criminal infraction; CR = criminal case; CV
- = civil case; FA = family case; MI = motor vehicle infraction; MV = motor vehicle case; SC = small claims.

- **Domicile:** The permanent home of a person. A person may have several residences, but only one domicile.

- **Drug Court:** A special session of the superior court that is responsible for hearing cases involving charges of drug offences.

- **Education Program:** A program for family violence offenders that, if granted and successfully completed, results in dismissal of criminal charges (C.G.S 46B – 38C).

- **Ejectment**: A legal case filed against someone who is a holdover tenant (someone who remains after the expiration of a lease).

- **Electronic Monitoring**: An electronic system that provides the Probation Officer or Bail Commissioner a report about whether the offender has left home during the time when the offender was required to remain at his or her home.

- **Emancipated Minor:** A person under the legal majority age of 18 who is granted most rights and legal privileges of an adult (C.G.S 46B-150, et seq.).

- **Emancipation**: The release of a youth from the legal authority and control of the youth's parents and the corresponding release of the youth's parents from their obligations to the youth.

- **Eminent Domain:** The legal process by which private property is taken for public use without the consent of the owner.

- Eviction: Legally forcing a tenant out of rented property (Housing Publications).

- **Evidence**: Testimony, documents or objects presented at a trial to prove a fact.

- **Ex-parte**: Done for, or at the request of, one side in a case only, without prior notice to the other side.

- **Execution Suspended**: A prison sentence that is suspended in whole or in part provided certain conditions of probation or conditional discharge are met by the defendant.

- **Failure to Appear**: In a civil case, failing to file an appearance form. In a criminal case, failing to come to court for a scheduled hearing.

- **Family Relations Counselor**: A person who mediates disagreements and negotiates agreements in custody, visitation and divorce cases. At the request of the judge, a family relations counselor may evaluate a family situation by interviewing each parent and the children in the family. The family relations counselor then writes a report for the judge, making recommendations about custody and visitation. Works in the family Services Office.

- **Family Support Magistrate**: A person who decides cases involving child support and paternity. Can also enforce court orders involving paternity, child support and alimony.

- **Family Violence Education Program**: A program for family violence offenders that if successfully completed, results in the dismissal of criminal charges.

- **Family Violence Victim Advocate**: A person who works with domestic violence victims to determine their needs and inform them of their rights and resources available to them.

- **Family with Service Needs:** Also called FWSN. A family that includes a child, who (a) runs away without just cause, (b) is beyond the control of his/her parents/guardian, (c) has engaged in indecent or immoral conduct, and/or (d) is a truant or continuously defiant of school rules and regulations.

- **Felony**: Any criminal offense for which a person may be sentenced to a term of imprisonment of more than one year.

- **Felony Murder**: A murder committed while the person is also committing a felony.

- **Filing**: Giving the court clerk legal papers which become part of the case file.

- **Financial Affidavit**: Short / Long – A sworn statement of income, expenses, property (called assets) and debts (called liabilities).

- **Finding**: The court's or jury's decision on issues of fact.

- **Foreclosure**: A court order ending the legal ownership of property.

- **Foreman**: An elected member of a jury who delivers the verdict to the court.

- **Garnishment**: A court order to collect money or property. For example, a garnishment may be issued to an employer to pay part of an employee's wages to someone else to pay a debt or judgment.

- **GA – Geographical Area**: The court location where motor vehicle and most criminal cases are heard. There are 22 Geographical Areas in Connecticut.

- **Grievance**: A complaint filed against an attorney or judge, claiming an ethics violation.

- **Guardian**: A person who has the power and duty to take care of another person and/or to manage the property and rights of another person who is considered incapable of taking care of his or her personal affairs.

- **Guardian Ad Litem**: A person, usually a parent, appointed by the court to represent a child or unborn person in a court case. If a family member is not available, a judge may appoint an attorney.

- **Habeas Corpus**: A court order used to bring a person physically before a court in order to test the legality of the person's detention. Usually, it is directed to the official or person detaining another, commanding him to bring the person to court for the judge to determine if that person has been denied liberty without due process of law.

- **Hearsay**: Testimony given by a witness who tells second or third hand information.

- **Honor Court**: A program of outpatient group therapy for alcohol abusers.

- **Housing Specialist**: A person who provides pretrial mediation of landlord/tenant cases to reach settlement. Also provides information about community resources to litigants.

- **Hung Jury**: A jury whose members cannot reconcile their differences of opinion and thus cannot reach a verdict.

- **Incarceration**: Confinement to a state correctional institute or prison.

- **Income Withholding Order**: A court order to deduct child support or alimony payments from someone's wages. All child support court orders must include an income withholding order unless both parents ask the judge not to.

- **Indigent**: Someone without enough money to either support himself or herself or his or her family. Someone who cannot afford to pay certain fees required by the court. (Civil, Family, Housing / Juvenile).

- **Information (the)**: In a criminal case, the formal court document in the clerk's file, which contains the charges, dates of offenses, bond status, continuance dates and disposition.

- **Infraction**: A case where the fine may be paid by mail and usually the person does not have to appear or come to court. For example, a speeding ticket(Infractions Schedule).

- **Injunction**: A court order to stop doing or to start doing a specific act.

- **Interpreter**: The person who correctly translates court hearings from a second language to English. An interpreter is provided at no cost to the person who needs the interpreter in all cases where the person's life, freedom, children or housing are at risk of being taken away. Interpreters are also provided for criminal and child support cases.

- **Interrogatory**: Formal, written questions used to get information from another party in a lawsuit.

- **Investigatory Grand Jury**: A judge, constitutional state referee or any three judges of the Superior Court, appointed by the Chief Court Administrator to conduct and investigation into the commission of a crime or crimes.

- **Judge**: A person who hears and decides cases for the courts. Appointed by the governor for a term of eight years and confirmed by the General Assembly.

- **Judgment**: A court decision. Also called a decree or an order.

- **Judgment File**: A permanent court record of the court's final disposition of the cast JD-Judicial District: Connecticut has 13 judicial districts (JD) in which civil, criminal, family and juvenile matters are heard. Civil jury, civil non-jury administrative appeals and family matters generally are heard in a JD courthouse.

- **Juris Number**: An identification number assigned to each attorney in Connecticut.

- **Jurisdiction**: Power and authority of a court to hear and make a judgment in a case.

- **Juror**: Member of a jury.

- **Jury Charge**: The judge's formal instructions on the law to the jury before it begins deliberations.

- **Jury instructions**: Directions given by the judge to the jury concerning the law of the case. (Civil/Criminal).

- **Juvenile Court**: Also called Superior Court for Juvenile Matters. A special division of the Superior Court designated to hear all cases concerning uncared for, dependent children and youth and delinquents. All juvenile court proceedings and case records are confidential and are not public information.

- **Juvenile Delinquent**: A person under the age of 16 who commits a criminal act.

- Juvenile Detention: State facility to provide for the temporary care of a child who alleged to be delinquent and who requires a physically restricted, secure environment.

- **Juvenile Detention Center**: A secure facility for juveniles operated by the Division of Juvenile Detention Services of the Connecticut Judicial Branch, open 24hours a day, 7days a week.

- **Juvenile Detention Officer**: Also called JDO. A person who works within a Juvenile Detention Center.

- **Juvenile Matters**: All cases concerning unscarred for neglected or dependent children and youth termination of parental rights of children committed to a state agency, matters concerning families with service needs, contested matters involving termination of parental rights or removal of guardian transferred from the probate court and the emancipation of minors. I does not include guardianship or adoption cases, or adoption cases, or matters affecting property rights of any child or youth over which Probate Court has jurisdiction. The probate Court hears appeals concerning adoption, termination of parental rights and removal of a parent as guardian are included. Juvenile matters in the criminal session include all cases concerning delinquent children in the state.

- **Juvenile Probation**: Placement of a adjudicated delinquent under the supervision of a juvenile probation officer.

- **Juvenile Transportation Officer**: Also called JTO. A person who provides safe transportation services for juveniles in custody.

- **Law librarian**: Court staff who maintain legal reference and research materials for public use.

- **Legal Aid or legal Services**: Free legal representatives in civil cases for income eligible persons.

- **Legal Custody**: Relationship with a child created by court order which gives a person legal responsibility for the physical possession of a minor and the duty to protect, care for and discipline the child.

- **Legal Separation**: A court order describing the conditions under which two married people will live separately.

- **Lien**: A charge, hold, or claim upon property of another as security for a debt.

- **Lis Pendens**: A pending lawsuit. Jurisdiction or control that courts have over property in a case waiting for final disposition. A notice of lis pendens is filed on the land records.

- **Litigant**: A party to a case.

- **Lockout**: Illegally forcing a tenant out of rented property, usually by changing the locks on the doors.

- **Magistrate**: A person who is not a judge but who is authorized to heart and decide certain types of cases. For example, family support magistrates hear cases involving child support.

- **Mandamus**: An order directed to a private corporation, or any of its officers or to a lower court commanding the performance of a particular act.

- **Marshal**: The persons responsible for courthouse security including the metal detectors at the entrance of each courthouse and maintaining order in each courtroom. A marshal can also serve (give copies of) legal papers to the other people named in a lawsuit.

- **Mediation**: A dispute resolution process in which an impartial third party assists the parties to voluntarily reach a mutually acceptable settlement.

- **Minor**: A person under age 18, the age of legal majority.

- **Misdemeanor**: A crime that carries a maximum penalty of one year and/or a 2,000 fine.

- **Mitigating Circumstances**: Circumstances that may be considered to reduce the guilt of a defendant. Usually based on fairness or mercy.

- **Mittimus Judgment**: Also called a Mitt. The formal document prepared by the court clerk to present a convicted defendant in a criminal case to the Department of Correction for Incarceration.

- **Modification**: Request to change a prior order usually requires showing a change in circumstances since the date of the prior order.

- **Motion**: Usually written request to the court in a case. Filed with the clerk's office.

- **Movant**: The person who filed the motion, or request to the court in a case.

- **Ne Excel**: Legal paper requesting that a person be required to remain within the jurisdiction of the court (either through incarceration or posting of a bond).

- **Neglected Minor**: A child or youth who has (a) been abandoned, (b) is being denied proper attention (c) is being permitted to live under condition injurious to his/her wellbeing, or (d) has been abused.

- **No Contact Order**: A court order that prohibits contact by a defendant with a victim; can be ordered by a judge, a bail commissioner, a probation officer or a parole officer.

- **No Fault Divorce**: The most common kind of divorce, where no one needs to prove that the husband or the wife is at fault, or caused the marriage to end. Described as "broken down irretrievably".

- **Nolle**: Short for nolle prosequi, which means "no prosecution". A disposition of a criminal or motor vehicle case where the prosecutor agrees to drop the case against the defendant but keeps the right to the next thirteen months. The nolle is entered on the court record and the defendant is released from custody. If the defendant stays out of trouble during the thirteen months, the case is removed from the official court records.

- **Nolo Contendere**: It means "No contest". A plea in a criminal case that allows the defendant to be convicted without admitting guilt for the crime charged. Although a finding of guilty is entered on the criminal court record; the defendant can deny the charges in a civil action based on the same acts.

- **No Contest**: A plea in a criminal case that allows the defendant to be convicted without admitting guilt for the crime charged. Also called nolo contender. Although a finding of guilty is entered on the criminal court record, the defendant can deny the charges in a civil action based on the same acts.

- **Non-Suit**: Vacating a case by the court, usually for failure to prosecute.

- **Notarize**: To formally complete a document by acknowledgement or oath.

- **Oath**: To swear/affirm to the truth of a statement/document.

- **Office of Adult Probation**: A division within the Judicial Branch. The primary responsibilities of the Office of Adult Probation are to supervise persons placed on probation, to conduct investigations for the court to provide background information on convicted offenders and to conduct eligibility investigations for special programs.

- **Order**: A written direction of a court of judge to do or refrain from doing certain acts.

- **Order to Detain**: An order signed by a judge of the Superior Court authorizing admission of a juvenile to a Juvenile Detention Center, pending a hearing on the next business day.

- **Order of Detention (Detention Order)**: An order issued by a judge of the Superior Court finding that there is probable cause that a juvenile committed an offense or a violation of a court and ordering that the juvenile be held in a Juvenile Detention Center or some alternative facility until further order of the court.

- **Orders of Temporary Custody**: Also called an OTC. Court order placing a child or youth in the short-time legal custody of an individual or agency authorized to care for juveniles.

- **Parcel**: A tract or a plot of land.

- **Parenting Education Program**: A mandatory program for persons involved in a divorce with children or a custody or visitation case. Must be attended within 60 days of the return date on the summons.
- **Parole**: Release from incarceration after serving part of a sentence.

- **Parties**: The people or legal entities that named as plaintiff(s) and defendant(s) on legal papers.

- **Party**: A person or legal entity that is named as a plaintiff or defendant on legal papers.

- **Paternity**: Legal fatherhood.

- **Pendent elite order**: A court order made before final orders are granted.

- **Peremptory Challenge**: The rejection of a prospective juror by the attorneys in a case, without having to give a reason. State law defines the number of peremptory challenges available.

- **Perjury**: Making false statements under oath.

- **Petition**: A formal written request to a court, which starts a special proceeding. In juvenile court, the legal document which specifies the complaint against the juvenile and/or family; it includes the name, age and address of the minor and his/her guardian, as well as the statutory grounds and facts upon which the request for the court intervention is based.

- **Petitioner**: Another word for plaintiff, the person starting the lawsuit.

- **Plaintiff**: the person who sues or starts civil case, also called the petitioner or the complainant.

- **Plea**: An accused persons answer to a criminal charge. For example; not guilty; guilty; no contest.

- **Plea Bargain**: The agreement a defendant make with the prosecutor to avoid a trial. Usually involves pleading guilty to lesser charges in exchange for a lighter sentence.

- **Pleadings**: The court documents filed with the court by the parties in a civil or criminal case. For example motion to dismiss; motion for modification.

- **Posting Bond**: To pay the court ordered bond amount with cash or property.

- **Post Judgment**: Any request to a court or action by a judge after a judgment in a case.

- **Practice Book**: Contains the rules of court and forms which **must** be followed in all Connecticut court cases. Available in all courthouse law libraries.

- •

- **Pre-Sentence Investigation**: Also called PSI. A background investigation conducted by a probation officer on a person who has been convicted of a criminal offense.

- **Pretrial**: In a civil case, a conference with a judge or trial referee to discuss discovery and settlement. In a criminal case, a conference with the prosecutor, defense attorney and judge to discuss the case status and what will happen next.

- **Pretrial Hearing**: Conference with attorneys to determine scope of possible trial with view toward resolving issues through agreement.

- **Probable Cause Hearing**: A hearing held before a judge in criminal cases to determine if enough evidence exists to prosecute. The probable cause hearing must be conducted within 60 days of the filing of the complaint or information in Superior Court, unless the accused person waives the time or the court grants an extension based on good cause.

- **Probate/Probate Court**: A court with limited authority to hear certain kinds of cases, such as adoption, guardianship, mental health commitments. Not a part of the Superior Court system.

- **Probation**: When a convicted offender receives a suspended term of incarceration and is the supervised by a probation officer for a period of time set by a judge.

- **Probation Absconder**: A person under probation supervision whose location unknown, in violation of the conditions of their probation.

- **Promise to Appear**: A type of non-financial bond where the defendant agrees to return to court without giving cash or property.

- **Pro Se**: A latin phrase meaning for "yourself"—representing yourself in any kind of case.
- **Pro se Divorce**: Do it yourself divorce – (en epanol).

- **Prosecute**: To carry on a case or judicial proceeding. To proceed against a person criminally.
- **Prosecutor**: Also called the state's attorney. Represents the state in a criminal case against a defendant.
- **Protective Order**: A criminal court order issued by a judge to protect a family or household member.
- **Public Defender**: An attorney appointed and paid by the state who defends a person in a criminal case after the court finds that the person in a criminal case after the court finds that the person is indigent-financially unable to hire a private attorney.
- **Ready**: Means ready to start the trial or begin oral argument. Usually said by an attorney or party in response to a judge calling the list of scheduled cases.
- **Record**; The pleadings, the exhibits and the transcript made by the court reporter of all proceedings in a trial.

- **Referee**: Judges who reach the mandatory retirement age of 70 may be designated as Judge Trial Referees by the Chief Justice and can hear and decide certain types of cases.
- **Regional Child Protection Docket**: A specialized court designed to hear complicated child protection cases. One judge hears the case from start to finish. Located in Middletown.

- **Regional Family Trial Docket**: A specialized court designed to hear complicated child protection cases. One judge hears the case from start to finish. Located in Middletown.
- **Residential Treatment Programs**: Programs that provide extensive drug or alcohol treatment on an inpatient basis.
- **Respondent**: Another word for defendant: The person responding to a lawsuit. In Juvenile court, the word refers to the person or persons name in a petition. When used in Practice Book Sec. 2-29 through 2-62 the word "respondent' shall mean the attorney against whom a grievance complaint or presentment has been filed or a person who is alleged to have been engaged in the unauthorized practice of law pursuant to General Statures § 51-88."
- **Rest**: To be done presenting the evidence in a case as in "the plaintiff rests".
- **Restitution**: Money ordered to be paid by the defendant to the victim to reimburse the victim for the costs of the crime. Generally making good, or giving the equivalent for any loss, damage or injury caused by a persons actions. Often a condition of probation.
- **Restraining Order**: A civil court order to protect a family or household member from the physical abuse.
- **Return Date**: The date on which the 90-day waiting period for a divorce begins. Also, the date tat starts the countdown for

things taking place in a case, including the deadlines for filing certain papers including the state by which the defendant should file an appearance. Nothing happens in court on the return date and no one needs to go to court on the return dat.

- The return date is always a Tuesday in civil and family cases. In summary process (eviction) cases, the return date is any week day, Monday through Saturday, except a holiday, usually 7 to 10 days from the date the clerk signs the summons if the summons is signed by the clerk.

- **Revocation Hearing**: A hearing held before a judge to determine whether or not a person has violated the conditions of probation. If there is a finding that a violation has occurred, the judge may impose all or part of the original sentence.

- **Rule to Show Cause**: Summons compelling a person to appear in court on a specific date to answer to a request that certain be modified or vacated.

- **Seal**: A court order closing a case file from public review, usually in cases of youthful offenders and acquittal. Prevents the public from obtaining information on the cases.

- **Senior Judge**: A judge who reaches the age of 65, or who meets certain other requirements and chooses senior status. Senior judges hear cases on a part time basis until the y reach the mandatory retirement age of 70.

- **Sentences**: The penalty imposed by a judge after the defendant is convicted of a crime. Sentences can be: Concurrent – Multiple sentences will be served at the same time (i.e., sentences of 10 years, 8 years and 2 years – to be served concurrently – equal a total effective sentence of 10 years.) Consecutive – The sentences are served back-to-back. The same example above would equal a total effective existence 20 years.

- **Sentencing**: When a criminal defendant is brought before judge after conviction for ordering the terms of the punishment.

- **Sentence Modification**: A defendant's written application to the sentencing judge or court to reduce the sentence at any time during the sentence. The judge conducts a hearing. If the original sentence was more than three years, the prosecutor must agree.

- **Sentence Review**: A defendant's written application to a three judge panel to review the sentence. Must be filed within 30 days after being sentenced with the court clerk. A review decision can increase or decrease the sentence.

- **Serious Juvenile Offender**: A child who has been adjudicated by the juvenile court for a serious juvenile offense.

- **Serious Juvenile offense**: Certain criminal offenses listed in the Connecticut General Statutes, which are crimes against persons, serious property crimes and certain drug offenses. A juvenile charged with a Serious Juvenile Offense by police may be admitted to a Juvenile Detention Center with a prior court order may be released only by order of a judge of the Superior Court.

- **Service**: The legal method for gibing a copy of the court papers being filed to their parties in a case.

- **Short Calendar**: A list of cases in which hearing by the judge or magistrate is requested or required.

- **Slip Opinions**: Opinions, or written decisions, of the Supreme Court or the Appellate Court that are publicly released prior to their official publication in the Connecticut Law Journal.

- **Special Sessions of the Superior Court**: A program of the Judicial Branch where cases of a single type are heard by the same judge through the entire case for example: Drug Session; Tax Session Community Court.

- **State Referee**: A retired judge who presides over cases referred by the court with agreement of counsel for both parties. Has full powers of an active trial judge.

- **States Attorney**: An attorney who represents the state in criminal cases. The prosecutor.

- **Statue**: A law enacted by a legislative body.

- **Statute of Limitations**: A certain time allowed by law for starting a case. For example, six years in a; contract case.

- **Stay**: Temporarily stopping a judicial proceeding.

- **Stipulation**: A command to appear in court to testify.

- **Subpoena Duces Tecum**: A legal paper requiring someone to produce documents or records for a trial.

- **Substance Abuse Education**: A community-based program for drug offenders that provides education about the harmful effects of drug abuse and supervises community service.

- **Substitute Charge**: In a criminal case, a charge that replaces the original charge by the prosecutor.

- **Summons**: A legal paper that is used to start a civil case and get jurisdiction over a party.

- **Summons (Juvenile)**: A written notice issued by the court commanding a person to appear in a court at a given date and time. A summons is issued to an individual charged or other party on a petition or complaint.

- **Support Enforcement Officer**: A person who supervises child support payments and brings parent to cover to enforce child support orders. May also file legal papers to modify or change child support orders.

- **Testimony**: Statements made by a witness or party under oath.

- **Time Served**: A sentence of incarceration equal to the amount of time a defendant has already spent in state custody waiting for disposition of the case.

- **Tithe**: Legal recognition of the ownership of property, usually proven by a document.

- **Tort**: A civil injury or wrong to someone else, or their property.

- **Transcript**: The official written record of everything that was said at a court proceeding, a hearing, or a deposition.

- **Transfer**: Assignment of a case to another court location by court order.

- **Transfer Hearing**: Juvenile Court hearing to determine whether a child, 14 or older, charged with a serious juvenile offense should have his/her case transferred to a criminal court and be subject to the same processes and penalties as an adult charged with the same crime.

- **Trial De Noyo**: A new trial or retrial in which the whole case with evidence and witnesses is presented as if no previous trial had been held.

- Trial Referee: An attorney appointed by the Chief justice to hear any civil non-jury case where the parties agree to use a trial referee, and all the legal papers have been filed.

- **Uncared For**: Legal description of a child or youth who is homeless or whose home cannot provide the specialized care which his/her physical, emotional or mental condition requires.

- **Unconditional Discharge**: A sentence in a criminal case in which the defendant is released without imprisonment, probation supervision or conditions.

- **Vacate**: To cancel or rescind a court order.

- **Venue**: The court location.
- **Victim Services Advocate**: A person who assesses a victim's needs and helps the victim understand the court case, how to exercise their rights and how to access other resources.
- **Visitation**: A court order deciding the amount of time a non-custodial parent may spend with his or her child, also called parenting time or access.
- **Violation**: An offense for which the only sentence authorized is a fine.
- **Violation of Probation**: Action or inaction that disobeys a condition of probation.
- **Voir Dire**: "To speak the truth." The process of questioning prospective jurors or witnesses about their qualifications.
- **Wage withholding**: A court order to deduct child support or alimony payment from someone's wage. All child support court orders must include an income withholding order unless both parents ask the judge not to.
- **Witness**: A person who testifies to what they saw, heard observed or did.
- **Youth**: Any person sixteen (16) to eighteen (18) years of age.
- **Youthful Offender**: The legal status of persons who have been arrested for a crime committed when they were between the ages

of 16 and 18 and who meet another requirement. All 16- and 17-year-old defendants are treated as youthful offenders, except those who have been charged with certain felonies have already been convicted of a felony on the adult docket or have been adjudicated as a serious juvenile offender. For defendants treated as Youthful Offenders, the information and proceeding are confidential and do not become a part of the person's criminal record.

## Legal Vocabulary 2.

| A | Burden Of Proof | Cross-Examination | F | Indictment |
|---|---|---|---|---|
| Acquit | | Custody | Family Law | Infraction |
| Affidavit | C | D | Felony | Injunction |
| Aid And Abet | Capital | Damages | Fiduciary | Innocent |
| Allegation | Crime | Decree | Fraud | Instruction |
| Appeal | Case | Defendant | G | J |
| Appearance | Case Law | Defense | Grand Jury | Jail |
| Argument | Chambers | Deposition | Grievance | Judge |
| Arrest | Claim | Disbarment | Guardian | Judiciary |
| Assault | Circumstantial Evidence | Docket | Guardianship | Jurisdiction |
| Attorney | Complainant | Due Process | | Jury |
| B | Complaint | E | Guilty | Justice |
| Bail | Confess | Entrapment | H | L |
| Bail Bond | Confession | Equity | Habeas Corpus | Larceny |
| Bailiff | Constitution | Escrow | Hearing | Law Lawsuit |
| Bankrupt | Al Law | Estate | Hearsay | Lawyer |
| Bankruptcy | Contract | Ethics | Hung Jury | Legal |
| Bar | Continuance | Evidence | | Legislation |
| Bar Exam | Counsel | Examination | | Leniency |
| Bench Warrant | Court | Exonerate | I | Liable |

| Bond | Crime | Expunge | Immunity | Lien |
|---|---|---|---|---|
| Booking | Criminal | Power Of Attorney | Incarceration | Litigant |
| M | Opinion | | Incompetent | Litigation |
| Manslaughter | Order | | V | |
| Marshal | Ordinance | | Vacate | |
| Mediation | | | Venue | |
| Minor | P | | Verdict | |
| Misdemeanor | Paralegal | | W | |
| Mistrial | Pardon | | Waiver | |
| Moot | Parole | | Warrant | |
| Murder | Party | | Willwitness | |
| N | Perjury | | Writ | |
| Negligence | Petition | | Z | |
| O | Plaintiff | | Zoning | |
| Oath | Plea | | | |
| Objective | Plea Bargain | | | |

## MIND YOUR ENGLISH SERIES

*BY: Magnus Oku*

1. Improve on your English sentences: Mind your English Series 1
2. The writing process – Get it right from the start Mind your English Series 2
3. Composition and real English Grammar Mechanics: Mind your English Series 3

# ABOUT THE AUTHOR

Magnus Oku, an acclaimed author, speaker, documentary producer and filmmaker, holds degrees in English Literature and Communication. His literary prowess has earned him significant recognitions since 2007, with many of his stories and scripts adapted into successful films. Renowned for his visual storytelling, he excels as a director and producer, bringing his literary creations to life on the big screen.

His influence extends to academia, where he shares his knowledge as a lecturer of English, Literature, and Communications, passionately imparting his wisdom and wealth of experience.

Recipient of prestigious awards, including the African Peace Awards for Media Excellence (Ghana). His global impact is evident in his management deal with Passion Inspired USA. This partnership ensures the widespread promotion of his literary content worldwide. He is the MD of Artlife Media, Magnus Oku Books, and National Coordinator of Nation Builders and Reformers Organisation (NBRO) in Nigeria.

# ABOUT THE BOOK

Unlock the power of effective communication with **"Mind Your English".** This book is your essential companion on the journey to mastering English sentences. In this text, correctness meets creativity in communication as you learn to articulate your thoughts with precision and finesse. Whether you're aiming to excel in writing or spoken discourse, "Mind Your English" offers invaluable insights and practical tips to elevate your language skills to new heights.

Discover the joy of speaking correctly as you navigate through engaging exercises and illuminating examples. With Oku's guidance, language learning becomes not just a task, but a delightful adventure. Say goodbye to confusion and embrace clarity with "Mind Your English." Let's embark on this enriching journey together!

www.ingramcontent.com/pod-product-compliance
Lightning Source LLC
LaVergne TN
LVHW050317160826
845677LV00014B/3439

* 9 7 8 9 7 8 5 5 5 9 6 0 6 *